REGENTS RESTORATION DRAMA SERIES

General Editor: John Loftis

ALL FOR LOVE

JOHN DRYDEN

ALL FOR LOVE

Edited by

DAVID M. VIETH

UNIVERSITY OF NEBRASKA PRESS · LINCOLN

MANUFACTURED IN THE UNITED STATES OF AMERICA

Regents Restoration Drama Series

The Regents Restoration Drama Series provides soundly edited texts, in modern spelling, of the more significant plays of the late seventeenth and early eighteenth centuries. The word "Restoration" is here used ambiguously and must be explained. A strict definition of the word is unacceptable to everyone, for it would exclude, among many other plays, those of Congreve. If to the historian it refers to the period between 1660 and 1685 (or 1688), it has long been used by the student of drama in default of a more precise term to refer to plays belonging to the dramatic tradition established in the 1660s, weakening after 1700, and displaced in the 1730s. It is in this extended sense—imprecise though justified by academic custom—that the word is used in this series, which includes plays first produced between 1660 and 1737. Although these limiting dates are determined by political events, the return of Charles II (and the removal of prohibitions against operation of theaters) and the passage of Walpole's Stage Licensing Act, they enclose a period of dramatic history having a coherence of its own in the establishment, development, and disintegration of a tradition.

The editors have planned the series with attention to the projected dimensions of the completed whole, a representative collection of Restoration drama providing a record of artistic achievement and providing also a record of the deepest concerns of three generations of Englishmen. And thus it contains deservedly famous plays—*The Country Wife*, *The Man of Mode*, and *The Way of the World*—and also significant but little known plays, *The Virtuoso*, for example, and *City Politiques*, the former a satirical review of scientific investigation in the early years of the Royal Society, the latter an equally satirical review of politics at the time of the Popish Plot. If the volumes of famous plays finally achieve the larger circulation, the other volumes may have the greater utility, in making available texts otherwise difficult of access with the editorial apparatus needed to make them intelligible.

The editors have had the instructive example of the parallel and senior project, the Regents Renaissance Drama Series; they have in fact used the editorial policies developed for the earlier plays as their own, modifying them as appropriate for the later period and as the experience of successive editions suggested. The introductions to the separate Restoration plays differ considerably in their nature. Although a uniform body of relevant information is presented in each of them, no attempt has been made to impose a pattern of interpretation. Emphasis in the introductions has necessarily varied with the nature of the plays and inevitably—we think desirably—with the special interests and aptitudes of the different editors.

Each text in the series is based on a fresh collation of the seventeenth- and eighteenth-century editions that might be presumed to have authority. The textual notes, which appear above the rule at the bottom of each page, record all substantive departures from the edition used as the copy-text. Variant substantive readings among contemporary editions are listed there as well. Editions later than the eighteenth century are referred to in the textual notes only when an emendation originating in some one of them is received into the text. Variants of accidentals (spelling, punctuation, capitalization) are not recorded in the notes except in instances in which they have, or may have, substantive relevance. Contracted forms of characters' names are silently expanded in speech prefixes and stage directions and, in the case of speech prefixes, are regularized. Additions to the stage directions of the copy-text are enclosed in brackets.

Spelling has been modernized along consciously conservative lines, but within the limits of a modernized text the linguistic quality of the original has been carefully preserved. Contracted preterites have regularly been expanded. Punctuation has been brought into accord with modern practices. The objective has been to achieve a balance between the pointing of the old editions and a system of punctuation which, without overloading the text with exclamation marks, semicolons, and dashes, will make the often loosely flowing verse and prose of the original syntactically intelligible to the modern reader. Dashes are regularly used only to indicate interrupted speeches, or shifts of address within a single speech.

Explanatory notes, chiefly concerned with glossing obsolete words and phrases, are printed below the textual notes at the bottom of each page. References to stage directions in the notes follow the admirable system of the Revels editions, whereby stage directions are keyed, decimally, to the line of the text before or after which they occur. Thus, a note on 0.2 has reference to the second line of the stage direction at the beginning of the scene in question. A note on 115.1 has reference to the first line of the stage direction following line 115 of the text of the relevant scene. Speech prefixes, and any stage directions attached to them, are keyed to the first line of accompanying dialogue.

JOHN LOFTIS

Stanford University

Contents

Regents Restoration Drama Series   v

List of Abbreviations   xi

Introduction   xiii

ALL FOR LOVE   1

Appendix A: Copies Collated   133

Appendix B: Chronology   135

List of Abbreviations

C1	Collected works, 1701
C2	Collected works, 1717
Noyes	George R. Noyes, ed. *Selected Dramas of John Dryden.* Chicago and New York, 1910.
om.	omitted
Q1	First quarto, 1678
Q2	Second quarto, 1692
Q3	Third quarto, 1696
Q4	Fourth quarto, 1703
Q5	Fifth quarto, 1709
S.D.	stage direction
S.P.	speech prefix

Introduction

The first edition of *All for Love, or The World Well Lost* (Q1), a quarto printed for Henry Herringman, was evidently published just after mid-March, 1678; it was entered, licensed by Roger L'Estrange, in the Stationers' Register on January 31, 1677/8, and was advertised in *The London Gazette* for March 21–25. The second quarto, 1692 (Q2), was printed from a copy of Q1 having all stop-press variants in the corrected state, and the third quarto, 1696 (Q3), was set from Q2. The fourth quarto of 1703 (Q4) is a page-for-page reprint of Q3, and the fifth quarto of 1709 (Q5) a page-for-page reprint of Q4. The text in Dryden's collected plays of 1701 (C1) was set from Q3. Congreve's text of 1717 (C2) was printed from a copy of Q1 having the outer forme of Sheet K in the uncorrected state.[1]

In the absence of evidence to the contrary, the only text possessing any authority appears to be Q1, which was printed with moderate care. In the present edition, which uses as copy-text the University of Illinois copy of Q1, all corrections in later editions are assumed to be no more than sensible guesswork by Dryden's contemporaries. Consequently, when they are preferred into the text, they are regarded as conjectural emendations. Variants are normally recorded only for Q2, Q3, and C1, those in Q4, Q5, and C2 being indicated, however, in a few cases of special interest. Obvious misprints such as turned letters are recorded somewhat more fully for Q1 than for Q2, Q3, or C1.[2]

---

[1] For bibliographical descriptions of the earliest editions of *All for Love*, see Hugh Macdonald, *John Dryden: A Bibliography* (Oxford, 1939), pp. 117–118, 148–153. For a list of later editions, see Carl J. Stratman, *Bibliography of English Printed Tragedy, 1565–1900* (Carbondale, Ill., 1966), pp. 169–171, and also "John Dryden's *All for Love:* Unrecorded Editions," *Papers of the Bibliographical Society of America*, LVII (1963), 77–79.

[2] Lists of the copies collated and of stop-press variants are given in Appendix A.

Few literary works have produced such a polarization of favorable and unfavorable opinions as has Dryden's *All for Love*.[3] On the positive side, countless audiences and readers have considered it Dryden's masterpiece in the drama and the finest of Restoration tragedies. It is, along with Congreve's *The Way of the World*, the best known of the Restoration plays. It has been called a "better play"[4] and more genuinely "tragic"[5] than its major source, Shakespeare's *Antony and Cleopatra*, as well as "the greatest—perhaps the only great—classical tragedy in English."[6]

Appealing to the Augustan taste for economy, propriety, and polish even while occasionally offending the Augustan moral sense, *All for Love* "drove Shakespeare's play from the stage during the eighteenth century." From 1700 to 1800 it enjoyed 123 performances, many by request of "persons of quality," "by command" of the royal family, or as benefits for actors and actresses who relied upon it to fill a playhouse.[7] Between 1702 and 1776 only eleven non-Shakespearean tragedies outranked it in popularity.[8] A lavish revival at Drury Lane in December of 1718 cost £600 for costumes, scenery, and decorations, apparently led Richard Steele to compose a prologue (which was not used),[9] and stirred the irascible John Dennis to condemn the play for

---

[3] They can be sampled in *Twentieth Century Interpretations of "All for Love,"* ed. Bruce King (Englewood Cliffs, N. J., 1968).

[4] L. P. Goggin, "This Bow of Ulysses," in *Essays and Studies in Language and Literature,* ed. Herbert H. Petit, Duquesne Studies, Philological Series 5 (Pittsburgh, 1964), p. 85.

[5] Bonamy Dobrée, *Five Restoration Tragedies* (London, 1928), p. xi; *Restoration Tragedy, 1660–1720* (Oxford, 1929), p. 90.

[6] Norman Suckling, "Dryden in Egypt: Reflexions on *All for Love,"* *Durham University Journal,* XLV (1952), 5.

[7] *British Dramatists from Dryden to Sheridan,* ed. George H. Nettleton, Arthur E. Case, and George Winchester Stone, Jr., 2d ed. (Boston, 1969), p. 72; *The London Stage,* ed. William Van Lennep et al. (Carbondale, Ill., 1960–1968), Parts 2–5.

[8] Emmett L. Avery, "The Popularity of *The Mourning Bride* in the London Theaters in the Eighteenth Century," *Research Studies of the State College of Washington,* IX (1941), 115–116.

[9] *The Occasional Verse of Richard Steele,* ed. Rae Blanchard (Oxford, 1952), pp. 50–51, 95.

immorality.[10] Thereafter, for a half-dozen years, it was produced regularly with Barton Booth playing Antony, John Mills Ventidius, Colley Cibber Alexas, Anne Oldfield Cleopatra, and Mary Porter Octavia.[11] In 1747 Spranger Barry appeared with distinction as Antony, and Peg Woffington as Cleopatra.[12] By contrast, David Garrick's production in 1759 of *Antony and Cleopatra*, the first recorded revival since Shakespeare's own time, had a limited success, with only six performances.[13]

Circumstances have contributed to the reputation of *All for Love* as Dryden's greatest play. At its premier performance in December of 1677, Dryden, forty-six years old, had attained full maturity as dramatist and poet. Of his twenty-eight plays, more than half, including all his heroic dramas and most of his best comedies, lay behind him. Now, so the popular legend goes, he cast off "his long-loved mistress, rhyme" and other shackling conventions of heroic drama to embrace the richness and flexibility of blank-verse tragedy. Not a hasty composition, *All for Love* was written during Dryden's two-year "retirement" from the stage after *Aureng-Zebe*, a leisurely interval which also brought forth his first great poem, *Mac Flecknoe*.[14] Robert Gould, in *The Play-House, A Satyr,* "Writ in the year 1685," felt obliged to grant that

> His *All for Love*, and most Correct of all,
> Of just and vast Applause can never fail,
> Never! . . .[15]

As if to foster the legend, Dryden remarked (in *A Parallel betwixt Painting and Poetry*, 1695) that whereas another of his plays "was given to the people," "I never writ anything for myself but

[10] *The Critical Works of John Dennis,* ed. Edward Niles Hooker (Baltimore, 1939–1943), II, 162–165.

[11] *The London Stage,* Part 2, pp. 517–518 et seq.; Thomas Davies, *Dramatic Miscellanies* (London, 1783–1784), II, 369–370.

[12] *The London Stage,* Part 3, p. 1284 et seq.

[13] George Winchester Stone, Jr., "Garrick's Presentation of *Antony and Cleopatra,*" *Review of English Studies,* XIII (1937), 20–38.

[14] *The Gyldenstolpe Manuscript Miscellany of Poems by John Wilmot, Earl of Rochester, and other Restoration Authors,* ed. Bror Danielsson and David M. Vieth, Stockholm Studies in English XVII (Stockholm, 1967), pp. 343–347.

[15] Quoted from Montague Summers, *The Restoration Theatre* (New York, 1934), pp. 307, 330.

Anthony and Cleopatra." Charles Gildon asserted that "the *All for Love* of Mr. *Dryden,* were it not for the false *Moral,* wou'd be a Masterpiece that few of the Ancients or Moderns ever equal'd."[16] Alexander Pope termed it "the most complete" English tragedy.[17]

Yet unfavorable judgments, never wholly lacking, have grown steadily more insistent. Even the earliest recorded performance of *All for Love* (probably not the premier), on December 12, 1677, at the Theatre Royal in Drury Lane, drew an audience of only 249 persons and receipts of £28 4s. The scantiness of theatrical records before 1700 renders conclusions hazardous, but only two later performances are known, on January 20, 1685/6 and May 9, 1694; other productions are suggested by the fact that the play was reprinted in 1692 and 1696.[18] Although Downes reports that at a performance in 1704 for Queen Anne's birthday, the Court was "very well pleas'd,"[19] Dennis claimed that before the revival of 1718, *All for Love* "had never brought four Audiences together."[20] Dr. Johnson deplored the "romantick omnipotence of Love" in Dryden's play, which he conceded grudgingly "is by universal consent accounted the work in which he has admitted the fewest improprieties of style or character."[21] By the late eighteenth century, *All for Love* had "gradually sunk into forgetfulness."[22]

In the twentieth century it has been cogently argued not only that the play itself and its subtitle, *The World Well Lost,* fail to follow the moralistic theory of tragedy adumbrated in Dryden's Preface, but that, oddly, the play would be poorer if it *had*

[16] *The Lives and Characters of the English Dramatick Poets . . . First begun by Mr. Langbain, improv'd and continued down to this Time, by a Careful Hand* (London, [1699]), Preface, sig. A5ᵛ.

[17] Joseph Spence, *Observations, Anecdotes, and Characters of Books and Men,* ed. James M. Osborn (Oxford, 1966), p. 207.

[18] *The London Stage,* Part 1, p. 265 and passim.

[19] John Downes, *Roscius Anglicanus,* ed. John Loftis, Augustan Reprint Society No. 134 (Los Angeles, 1969), p. 47.

[20] *Critical Works,* ed. Hooker, II, 164.

[21] *Life of Dryden,* in *Lives of the English Poets by Samuel Johnson,* ed. George Birkbeck Hill (Oxford, 1905), I, 361.

[22] Davies, *Dramatic Miscellanies,* II, 370.

followed the theory.[23] Dryden's characterization of Antony and Cleopatra has been judged weak beside Shakespeare's, and the unity of his plot has been criticized because so much action is initiated by other characters, particularly Alexas.[24] The imagery has been found deficient in immediacy and in the "iterative" or organic patterning necessary to make a play a poetic whole— hardly a minor flaw in a verse drama.[25]

Whatever its faults in comparison with Shakespeare, *All for Love* achieves, in terms of the neoclassical unities of time, place, and action, a tour de force whose craftsmanship is illuminated by contrast with *Antony and Cleopatra*. The decade spanned by Shakespeare's play, from 40 B.C. to the deaths of Antony and Cleopatra in August of 30 B.C., is compressed into Aristotle's "single revolution of the sun." In place of Shakespeare's settings scattered about the eastern Mediterranean, Dryden confines events to the Temple of Isis or nearby, achieving Corneille's *lieu théâtrale* or "indefinite place." Instead of a main plot with subplot, traditional in English drama, *All for Love* has one "main design," "without episode or underplot." Unlike Shakespeare's many short scenes, each scene is an entire act in *All for Love,* so that the question of *liaison des scènes,* or "joining of the scenes," never arises. Shakespeare's thirty-odd speaking parts are reduced to about one-third that number.

[23] Everett H. Emerson, Harold E. Davies, and Ira Johnson, "Intention and Achievement in *All for Love," College English,* XVII (1955), 84–87. See the reply by Bruce King, "Dryden's Intent in *All for Love," College English,* XXIV (1963), 267–271, and his *Dryden's Major Plays* (Edinburgh and New York, 1966), pp. 133–147.

[24] Hazelton Spencer, *Shakespeare Improved* (Cambridge, Mass., 1927), pp. 210–221; Ruth Wallerstein, "Dryden and the Analysis of Shakespeare's Techniques," *Review of English Studies,* XIX (1943), 165–185; Moody E. Prior, *The Language of Tragedy* (New York, 1947), pp. 192–211; Peter Nazareth, "*All for Love:* Dryden's Hybrid Play," *English Studies in Africa,* VI (1963), 154–163; A. D. Hope, "*All for Love,* or Comedy as Tragedy," in *The Cave and the Spring: Essays on Poetry* (Adelaide, Australia, 1965), pp. 144–163.

[25] F. R. Leavis, "*Antony and Cleopatra* and *All for Love," Scrutiny,* V (1936), 158–169; Kenneth Muir, "The Imagery of *All for Love," Proceedings of the Leeds Philosophical and Literary Society* (Literary and Historical Section), V (1940), 140–147; Otto Reinert, "Passion and Pity in *All for Love:* A Reconsideration," in *The Hidden Sense and Other Essays,* Maren-Sofie Røstvig et al. (Oslo, 1963), pp. 159–195.

Moreover, each act certainly concludes with a reversal or "turn." In despair over the loss of his Roman honor at Actium and his imagined loss of his Egyptian love, Cleopatra, Antony in Act I is persuaded by Ventidius to seek honor in a new battle. In Act II, addressed first by Alexas and then by Cleopatra, he recovers his love along with his honor as he sallies forth to military victory. The arrival of Dolabella and Octavia in Act III then forces him into exclusive recommitment to Roman values. The intrigues in Act IV develop the primary theme of *All for Love* by bringing out the true identities or "selves" of the main characters: Antony cannot rejoin Octavia because of his deep love for Cleopatra, Cleopatra cannot practice deceit to make Antony jealous, Dolabella realizes he was wrong in advising Antony to leave Cleopatra, Octavia prevaricates about the scene she has just witnessed between Cleopatra and Dolabella, and Ventidius's machinations make him look like a feeble copy of the schemer Alexas. Antony again feels he has lost both love and honor. In Act V, however, he and Cleopatra regain both through death.

Why should Dryden have ventured to adapt the very play which many readers regard as Shakespeare's greatest—which must also have seemed, among his tragedies, the one least easy to tailor to the three unities? It is futile to argue, as some have done, that Dryden's play must not be compared with Shakespeare's, for the latter is unforgettably the supreme expression of the historical myth of Antony and Cleopatra. Every successful new work in a literary tradition modifies, and is modified by, its predecessors; conversely, if the work is less than successful, it risks exposing its own poverty without enriching the tradition. The reader for whom Cleopatra is Shakespeare's "serpent of old Nile" might well object to Dryden's "silly, harmless, household dove."[26]

[26] Dryden's Cleopatra probably violates his own principle, invoked in his Preface to condemn Racine's Hippolytus, that a tragic dramatist "is bound to represent" "the particular characters of men, as we have them delivered to us by relation or history" (quoted from "The Grounds of Criticism in Tragedy" prefixed to *Troilus and Cressida*, 1679).

The explanation may lie in Dryden's technique of treating an earlier literary work, theme, genre, or subject as something more than a source but less than an allusion: more than a source because recognition of its presence is expected and enhances one's understanding of Dryden's work, less than an allusion because such recognition is not obligatory or necessary to understanding. This is properly "imitation," although the term unfortunately is vague and may connote some devices not ordinarily employed by Dryden. Seen this way, *All for Love* is like a giant metaphysical conceit in which elements of Shakespeare's sprawling play are yoked by violence together with the tighter concept of the three unities—"more exactly observed than, perhaps, the English theater requires," as Dryden wryly remarks in his Preface. Dryden's "imitation" of neoclassical dramatic form may have been his major motive in using Milton's *Samson Agonistes*.[27] Similarly, his "imitation" of *Antony and Cleopatra* is extended in at least three directions: in one direction through borrowings from other English plays on the same subject by Sir Charles Sedley, Thomas May,[28] and Samuel Daniel;[29] in a second through classical historical sources of the story such as Plutarch; and in a third through generous echoes of other plays by Shakespeare—perhaps the sense in which *All for Love* is claimed on its title page to be "written in imitation of Shakespeare's style." Other Shakespeare plays which have been mentioned include *Twelfth Night, As You Like It, Much Ado About Nothing, The Merchant*

[27] Morris Freedman, *"All for Love* and *Samson Agonistes," Notes and Queries,* CCI (1956), 514–517.

[28] H. Neville Davies, "Dryden's *All for Love* and Thomas May's *The Tragedie of Cleopatra Queen of Aegypt," Notes and Queries,* CCX (1965), 139–144, and "Dryden's *All for Love* and Sedley's *Antony and Cleopatra," Notes and Queries,* CCXII (1967), 221–227; Peter Caracciolo, "Dryden and the *Antony and Cleopatra* of Sir Charles Sedley," *English Studies,* L (1969), Anglo-American Supplement, 1–lv. Laurence Eusden insinuated that Dryden undertook *All for Love* to emulate Sedley's play.

[29] G. Thorn-Drury, "Some Notes on Dryden," *Review of English Studies,* I (1925), 79–80; *Dryden: The Dramatic Works,* ed. Montague Summers (London, 1932), IV, 528–530; *All for Love,* ed. Arthur Sale, 2d ed. (London, 1957), pp. 218–221; Muir, pp. 145–147.

of Venice, Julius Caesar, Richard II, Othello, Hamlet, Macbeth, and *Coriolanus.*[30]

Antony and Cleopatra may also have attracted Dryden because its resemblances to his own heroic plays promised an opportunity to repeat tested techniques of depicting a love-honor conflict amid the clash of differing cultures. Dryden, to be sure, barely approaches Shakespeare's marvelously ambivalent portrayal of the vaunted Roman honor, degenerating so readily into unscrupulous self-seeking, together with the debased sexuality of Egypt, out of which the exalted love of Antony and Cleopatra nevertheless burgeons. Antony vacillates like Almanzor, his situation suggests various besieged or moribund monarchs in Dryden's heroic plays,[31] and like the "irregularly great" Morat, he is a "Herculean hero." This type of figure is nearly superhuman or semi-divine, but his overabundance of vitality makes him undisciplined and potentially destructive even while it lifts him indefinably above the other characters.[32] In Dryden's Antony, who actually claims descent from Hercules, "his virtues lie so mingled with his crimes" as to be inseparable from them (III.49–51); his "vast soul" will not forgive "what as man he did/ Because his other parts are more than man" (I.125–133).

Indeed, Dryden's heroic plays, taken collectively, must be considered a separate area of "imitation" in *All for Love.* Essentially these are plays of ideas, not unlike George Bernard Shaw's; they aim to render tangible the abstract principles that were thought to guide human conduct. Lacking detailed psychological

[30] *"All for Love" and "The Spanish Fryar" by John Dryden,* ed. William Strunk, Jr. (Boston and London, 1911), p. xlv; T. P. Harrison, Jr., *"Othello* as a Model for Dryden in *All for Love,"* University of Texas *Studies in English,* No. 7 (1927), pp. 136–143; D. T. Starnes, "More About Dryden as an Adapter of Shakespeare," University of Texas *Studies in English,* No. 8 (1928), pp. 100–106, and "Imitation of Shakespeare in Dryden's *All for Love," Texas Studies in Literature and Language,* VI (1964), 39–46; Charles R. Forker, *"Romeo and Juliet* and the 'Cydnus' Speech in Dryden's *All for Love," Notes and Queries,* CCVII (1962), 382–383; S. Klima, "Some Unrecorded Borrowings from Shakespeare in Dryden's *All for Love," Notes and Queries,* CCVIII (1963), 415–418.

[31] *All for Love,* ed. R. J. Kaufman (San Francisco, 1962), p. xii.

[32] Eugene M. Waith, *The Herculean Hero* (New York, 1962).

delineation, individual characters tend to represent bundles of attitudes striving to operate within a matrix of moral obligations. In a typical scene, attention focuses upon overt analysis, in sharply pointed heroic couplets, of the abstract issues that should govern a specific decision, and then upon some character's capacity to act on this decision unless passion overcomes reason.[33]

Awareness of the intellectual nature of Dryden's heroic drama helps to account for the simplified, depersonalized characterization in *All for Love* in comparison with *Antony and Cleopatra*. More central to his play than Shakespeare's Antony, Dryden's protagonist is the intersection of a web of abstract obligations spun out from the secondary characters and partly indicated in the dramatis personae. Ventidius is Antony's "general" or spokesman for Roman honor, combining some functions of Shakespeare's Enobarbus, Ventidius, and Eros. Octavia, mother of "Antony's two little daughters," is his legal "wife." Dolabella, his "friend," recalls features of Shakespeare's Dolabella, Enobarbus, and Thidias. Cleopatra is Antony's mistress or representative of love, the devious traits of Shakespeare's heroine having been assigned to Alexas, who also exhibits aspects of Shakespeare's Alexas and Mardian the eunuch, and who epitomizes worldly "interest." In their quest for identity, Dryden's characters repeatedly seek general classifications to fit their roles. Antony rejects the designation of "emperor" (I.252–254, 273–277), Ventidius those of "father" (I.273) or "traitor" (I.378, 384–393), and Cleopatra those of "queen" (II.7) or a "wife" deserving only "respect" (II.76–82). Antony leaving for battle is a "soldier," not a "lover" (II.410–411); he labels Octavia "Caesar's sister" (III.255). Octavia and Cleopatra call themselves "Roman" and "queen" (III.418–419) but possess only "the specious title of a wife" and "the branded name of mistress" (III.460, 465). Dolabella and Cleopatra, Antony's "friend" and "mistress" of Act IV, are superseded in Act V by Ventidius and Cleopatra as his "friend" and "wife."

[33] Anne T. Barbeau, *The Intellectual Design of John Dryden's Heroic Plays* (New Haven, 1970). See also my "Concept as Metaphor: Dryden's Attempted Stylistic Revolution," *Language and Style*, III (1970), 197–204.

Techniques of heroic drama explain, without excusing, the most disconcerting passage in *All for Love*, in which Octavia pushes Antony's children to him:

VENTIDIUS.
  Was ever sight so moving? Emperor!
DOLABELLA.
  Friend!
OCTAVIA. Husband!
BOTH CHILDREN. Father!
ANTONY. I am vanquished. Take me,
  Octavia; take me, children; share me all. *Embracing them.*

(III.362–364)

Too often misunderstood as a clumsy bid for pathos, this incident objectively diagrams some of Antony's abstract obligations. As the second of three tableaux in Act III, the first being the ceremonial greeting of Antony and Cleopatra (III.0.1–6) and the third the confrontation between Cleopatra and Octavia, it typifies the unrealistic, ritualized style of the play as a whole.[34]

Another form of "imitation" in *All for Love* is the theme of "friendship," which is represented conspicuously by Dolabella and more briefly, near the beginning and end of the play, by Ventidius (e.g., V.318–334). Conventionally a subdivision of honor, the friendship motif is part of the common heritage of Western culture, descending ultimately from the classical *amicitia*, as illustrated in such famous pairs as Nisus and Euryalus. The theme is most familiar to English-speaking readers in various versions of the story of Palamon and Arcite, which provides a convenient paradigm. Usually two young men, bound together in friendship by like-minded honorable qualities, suffer a conflict when the passion of love overcomes one or both of them, often love for the same woman; they fight each other, and the untangling of their perplexities becomes a test of the storyteller's inventiveness. Dolabella and Antony never fight physically but otherwise enact

[34] Jean H. Hagstrum notes the play's "pictorial" or "iconic" quality in *The Sister Arts* (Chicago, 1958), pp. 184–197.

most steps of the paradigm. To the friendship theme Dryden has assimilated a device apparently originating in Shakespeare's use of Enobarbus to parallel Antony's conflict between honor and love. Initially a spokesman for Roman values, Enobarbus finds his worldly rationality increasingly conflicting with his affection for his doomed leader; after he subsequently deserts Antony, his realization that this action was a mistake implies that Antony should not leave Cleopatra. Similarly, in *All for Love*, Dolabella out of friendship persuades Antony to honor his Roman obligations; then, as his own love for Cleopatra reasserts itself, he reverses his earlier counsel.

The notion of using this device may actually have come from Nathaniel Lee's most popular play, *The Rival Queens, or The Death of Alexander the Great,* which should be considered a further basis of "imitation" in *All for Love*. First performed at the Theatre Royal on March 17, 1676/7, only nine months before Dryden's tragedy, *The Rival Queens* must have been specially present to the minds of Dryden's audience because the same actors created corresponding roles in the two plays.[35] Alexander and Antony were played by Charles Hart, noted for his regal bearing, and the "friend" in each instance, Lee's Hephestion and Dryden's Dolabella, by Thomas Clark; two years earlier, these actors had created a similar pair, Massinissa and Massina, in Lee's *Sophonisba*. Lee's Clytus, a blunt old-soldier spokesman for Macedonian values, and Dryden's Ventidius were acted by Michael Mohun. Cardell Goodman, Dryden's Alexas, had played Polyperchon, one of the conspirators headed by Cassander in *The Rival Queens*. Lee's virtuous queen Statira and Dryden's wifely Cleopatra were created by Elizabeth Boutell, whose petite stature, childlike look, and innocent manner must have type-cast her in 1675 for Wycherley's Margery Pinchwife.[36] Lee's Lysimachus and Dryden's Serapion, normative characters in somewhat different ways, were acted by Philip Griffin.

Besides their love-honor conflicts, *The Rival Queens* and *All for Love* depict a similar clash of cultures, in Lee's case between

[35] *The Rival Queens,* ed. P. F. Vernon (Lincoln, Nebr., 1970), p. xvi.

[36] *The History of the English Stage,* "By Mr. Thomas Betterton," generally attributed to Edmund Curll (London, 1741), p. 21.

Macedonian and Persian values. Both employ a type of structure, possibly suggested to Lee by the old Emperor in Dryden's *Aureng-Zebe* and used later by Addison in *Cato,* which centers upon a single overwhelming protagonist, to whom the lesser characters, either singly or in small groups, relate more directly through theme and action than they do to each other. Each protagonist, Alexander and Antony, is a "Herculean hero." To emphasize positive aspects in his very mixed character, he is contrasted with an anti-protagonist, Lee's Cassander and Dryden's Alexas. Not only did Lee antedate Dryden in adopting blank verse for his tragedy, but he may have given Dryden the idea of bringing his "rival queens," Octavia and Cleopatra, together on stage in Act III. Lee's use of Clytus to parallel Alexander recalls Enobarbus in *Antony and Cleopatra,* a play Lee knew well, and anticipates Dryden's Dolabella: having denounced Alexander's irrational weaknesses in comparison with Macedonian rationality and military virtue, Clytus shows his limited vision, and implies the breadth of Alexander's, by provoking his own death through his irrational weakness for wine.

One of several major shortcomings of *All for Love* results, however, from the friendship theme and Dryden's apparent use of *The Rival Queens:* its sanctioning of male homosexuality. Dolabella, "cast . . . in so soft a mold" (IV.12), is one "whom Caesar loves beyond the love of women" (III.85); Antony formerly "was his soul" (III.91) and greets him more fondly than "the young bridegroom, longing for his night" (III.121). The friendship theme, notwithstanding its frequent occurrence in Restoration drama, proved embarrassing. Unless the two young men were close blood relatives or shared some obvious self-interest, the implication of homosexuality, to the cynical Restoration mind, was well-nigh inescapable. Commonly the playwright's solution was to make them brothers. In *The Rival Queens,* the Alexander-Hephestion friendship is unabashedly homosexual, Clytus (even more than Ventidius) hates women, and Roxana is peculiarly masculine. Whatever Dryden's intentions were in *All for Love,* the trouble seems to be that although the Dolabella-Antony relationship provides logical parallels between these two characters, its psychological surge escapes the context of a play expressive of a civilization that has never, since classical times, really condoned homosexuality. How this homosexuality may reflect Dryden's real-life relationship with his young friend and future collaborator, Nathaniel Lee, remains unclear.

Several other interrelated weaknesses in *All for Love* result from the neoclassical unity of time. Because the play begins well after the climax of Antony's story, his former position as imperial ruler, as Shakespeare's "triple pillar of the world," is merely described, not dramatized. Thus he may seem to lack the stature of a tragic protagonist, an impression not improved by his first appearance in Act I in a posture of sentimental groveling. Normally, in a great tragedy, the protagonist's fate reaches out and affects the entire world of the play, but Dryden's Antony and Cleopatra retain so little control over public affairs that their experience is essentially private.[37] Since Antony's *hamartia* and his moment of fatal decision (at Actium?) are never acted out or even fully accounted for in retrospect, he seems scarcely responsible for his fate and strangely passive, vacillating under pressures from Ventidius, Alexas, Cleopatra, Dolabella, and Octavia. The play's language tends to be syntactically inert; its images of dreaming and sleep reflect the sense of suspended animation which suffuses the action.

The most damaging group of weaknesses in *All for Love* evidently stems from Dryden's emphasis in his heroic drama upon the abstract and general. In these plays, characters self-consciously analyze their emotional states rather than reveal them unconsciously in speech or action. Similarly, in *All for Love,* Antony's conflicts are externalized, and the emphasis is more moral than psychological. The action develops, in a sort of *psychomachia,* through a series of confrontations between the protagonist and various characters who semi-allegorically represent aspects of his situation. For this reason, even more than the foreshortening effect of the unity of time, Antony seems passive, weak, and lacking in stature, and the play as a whole seems excessively static and verbose. Dryden's techniques of abstraction are antithetical to the very nature of tragedy. They posit a relatively closed system of values which a character is expected to

[37] Stressed in Earl Miner, *Dryden's Poetry* (Bloomington, Ind., 1967), pp. 36–73.

comprehend and act upon. True tragedy, by contrast, usually entails a larger area of the irrational and inexplicable: the protagonist's sin unleashes a disproportionate amount of suffering, and the possibility of ultimate justice remains a vague hope beyond the grave. Moreover, the experience of the greatest tragic protagonists, unlike that of Dryden's Antony, is particularized, individual, and unique; there is only one Oedipus, one Lear, one Hamlet.

In the verse of *All for Love*, abstractness combines with deficiencies in the imagery to produce a verbal texture which is not so much poetry as ornamented prose, with insufficient concreteness and intensity for a fully realized tragedy.[38] One example must stand for many (italics mine):

> For if I stay one minute more to think
> How I am wronged, my *justice* and *revenge*
> Will cry so loud within me that my *pity*
> Will not be heard for either.
> (IV.534–537)

These are severe shortcomings; yet *All for Love* has some compensating strengths. Historically, it foreshadows uncannily the domestic tragedies and sentimental comedies of Dryden's successors—Cibber, Rowe, Steele, Lillo, Ibsen, Arthur Miller.[39] Because Antony's experience with Cleopatra, to whom (and Dolabella) he gave "half the globe . . ./ In dowry with my heart" (IV.484–485), is more private than public, these two resemble a husband and wife belonging to no particular social class. The issue separating them is in fact, if not legally, marital infidelity, and their situation is perilously close to comedy. Cleopatra's first words, "What shall I do, or whither shall I turn?" (II.1),

---

[38] This, I take it, is the real point of the discussion in Anne Davidson Ferry, *Milton and the Miltonic Dryden* (Cambridge, Mass., 1968), pp. 178–218.

[39] Baxter Hathaway, "John Dryden and the Function of Tragedy," *PMLA*, LVIII (1943), 665–673; Wallace Jackson, "Dryden's Emperor and Lillo's Merchant: The Relevant Bases of Action," *Modern Language Quarterly*, XXVI (1965), 536–544; Arthur C. Kirsch, *Dryden's Heroic Drama* (Princeton, 1965), pp. 128–133, 140–141; Selma Assir Zebouni, *Dryden: A Study in Heroic Characterization*, Louisiana State University Studies, Humanities Series No. 16 (Baton Rouge, 1965), pp. 50–59.

were to be echoed by countless female figures of suffering innocence in later sentimental dramas. Dryden's domestic emphasis
coincides with the principal theme of *All for Love,* the achievement of personal identity, which is merely incidental in *Antony
and Cleopatra.* Although Shakespeare's play questions what
Antony's true "self" is, its broader tragic concern is the fullest
possible experience of life—to be encompassed, paradoxically,
only by going out of life. Dryden's Cleopatra primarily discovers
her identity as Antony's "wife." Originally she disdains a "wife"
as "that thing,/ That dull, insipid lump, without desires,/ And
without pow'r to give 'em" (II.82–84). Her confrontation with
Octavia and attempt to make Antony jealous convince her, however, that though "fortune . . . has made a mistress of me,"
"Nature meant me/ A wife, a silly, harmless, household dove"
(IV.91–94). Death will make her "the bride of Antony" (V.463),
"his wife"; it will "knit our spousals with a tie too strong/ For
Roman laws to break" (V.412–418).

Another strength of *All for Love* is the ingenuity and origin-
ality of Dryden's characterization of the eunuch Alexas.[40] If
Antony, an ill-disciplined "Herculean hero," loses dignity through
his bungling attempts to reconcile love and honor (and even to
fall on his sword), Alexas's incapacity for either love or honor
emphasizes that Antony's problem is his excess of these positive
qualities. Alexas is "cast out from nature" (III.385); Antony is
"bounteous as nature; next to nature's God" (I.182). Whereas
Alexas dreads the "final separation" of his "two long lovers, soul
and body" (V.136–137), Antony and Cleopatra look forward to
joining one another in death. Alexas functions as a foil to other
characters such as Ventidius, whose narrowly Roman values too
easily lead to mere scheming. As self-justifying "interest"—indeed,
as means without ends—Alexas is finally most like Octavius, who
"knows no honor/ Divided from his int'rest" (III.212–213) and
who never appears on stage, his unseen presence inexorably
closing in upon the lovers like a symbol of the "world well lost."

Despite criticisms of the imagery of the play, at least three
image-patterns in *All for Love* have enough prominence and

[40] For possible sources, see Howard D. Weinbrot, "Alexas in *All for
Love:* His Genealogy and Function," *Studies in Philology,* LXIV (1967),
625–639.

consistency to be meaningful. Imagery of navigation, the sea (especially when stormy), and flowing fresh water generally suggests involvement in life. Antony has reached "my lowest watermark" and "the shipwrack of my fortunes" (III.129; II.318); Cleopatra, it is charged, will "let go her hold, and haste to shore,/ And never look behind" (II.387–389, 433–435). She is to use Dolabella like a fireship to ignite Antony's jealousy (IV.86–88). Alexas, accused of pushing her "boat to open sea, to prove,/ At my sad cost, if thou canst steer it back," insists he is pulling her to safety like "some shipwracked seaman near the shore,/ Dropping and faint with climbing up the cliff" (V.32–46). The Nile, the Mediterranean, Cleopatra on her barge, the sea-battle at Actium, and the desertion of the Egyptian fleet are constantly referred to. Fresh-water imagery can express inner states. Antony and Dolabella were close "as meeting streams" (III.95). In adversity, Antony draws upon "my native spring," which "lifts me to my banks" (III.132–134); his character is like "a shallow-forded stream,/ Seen to the bottom" (IV.438–439). Cleopatra's love, which distorts her reason "as what is straight seems crooked through the water" (II.86), has broken over "all the dams" and "drowned my heart" (IV.519–520). In the omens that begin the play, Antony and Cleopatra implicitly correspond to the sea-monsters stranded by the retreating flood, while the play's end secures them from "the storms of fate" (V.516).

A second pattern consists of images of commercial transactions, monetary value, and jewelry. Roman characters tend to view life in terms of bargain and sale. Octavius is a "usurer," fit only "to buy, not conquer, kingdoms" (III.214–215). Ventidius fears Antony's legions may be "sold" for the tear Cleopatra will "bid" (II.325–326). Antony, like a repentant Restoration rake, tells his Roman wife and children he has been "a thriftless debtor to your loves,/ And run out much, in riot, from your stock" (III.365–366). Later, bereft of "the least unmortgaged hope" (V.162), Antony spurns such "bribes of life" to die with Cleopatra (V.276), realizing that "my pow'r, my empire/ Were but my merchandise to buy her love,/ And conquered kings, my factors" (V.270–272). Cleopatra from the first sets love "above the price of kingdoms" (II.441–442), bestows jewels prodigally (II.183.1; II.200.1; III.411.S.D.), and finally herself becomes

Antony's "one dear jewel" (V.367), without whom the world is "an empty circle, since the jewel's gone" (V.274)—perhaps suggesting a ring. Combining commercial with water imagery, Antony compares himself to "a merchant roused/ From soft repose to see his vessel sinking,/ And all his wealth cast o'er" (V.206–208). Not Cleopatra, however, but "false Fortune, like a fawning strumpet," leaves "the bankrupt prodigal" Antony (V.85–88).

The third and most meaningful pattern, imagery of a child or infant, usually signifies failure to achieve a mature identity. Octavius is repeatedly "boy" (I.121; II.443; III.63; V.164), a status denied, however, to Alexas (III.382–392). To Ventidius, Antony's un-Roman behavior makes him a eunuch like Alexas (I.174) or an "infant" (II.235). After her self-image vis-à-vis Antony is unsettled by the *anagnorisis* of her confrontation with Octavia (III.458 ff.), Cleopatra retires to "weep,/ As harmless infants moan themselves asleep" (III.483–484). During Antony's similar problem of identity in Act IV, he reproaches Dolabella and Cleopatra for betraying "this tender heart, which with an infant fondness/ Lay lulled betwixt your bosoms" (IV.489–490). The pattern emerges in Dolabella's famous speech, "Men are but children of a larger growth" (IV.43–52). In his later lines, the most important in the play, he combines imagery of the child with water and monetary imagery to sum up Antony's plight:

> My friend, my friend!
> What endless treasure hast thou thrown away,
> And scattered, like an infant, in the ocean,
> Vain sums of wealth which none can gather thence!
> (IV.204–207)

Dryden retrieves some tragic effect at the end of *All for Love* through a device which, despite his simultaneous borrowings from Samuel Daniel, comes mainly from *Antony and Cleopatra*. Earlier in Dryden's play, as in Shakespeare's, Antony cannot bring together the conflicting claims of honor and love, of Rome and Egypt, because of "interest," which keeps the two lovers vulnerable to fate. With the empire lost, however, interest is replaced by a new third term that resolves all conflicts in a triple equation of love, honor, and death (to which Dryden awkwardly adds friendship in V.337–342). Committing suicide by a con-

ventional Roman method to preserve his honor, Antony nevertheless expects to rejoin his Egyptian love in death. Hoping
similarly to rejoin Antony, Cleopatra selects the Egyptian expedient of the asp, but death for her also means circumventing
the disgrace of being paraded through the Roman streets. Antony
dies kissing Cleopatra (V.401–402), and death for her is "like
my love" (V.442–445). She dies arrayed in her "crown and richest
jewels" (V.437) to meet Antony "as when I saw him first, on
Cydnos' bank," so that "my second spousals/ Shall match my
first in glory" (V.458–462).

All for Love as tragedy may have been a casualty of Dryden's
peculiar virtue as a writer, his ratiocinative power. If tragedy is
Man Suffering, Dryden is Man Thinking. Neither response to
life is necessarily superior to the other, but the rational and the
tragic may be radically incompatible.

THE PREFACE

As one of the greatest of English critics, John Dryden special-
ized in two sorts of endeavors. When writing straightforwardly,
particularly about earlier authors, he is remarkable for his
incisive judgments and his memorable way of stating them. On
other occasions, however, he is not above exploiting his formid-
able skills to pass off a faulty or unsuccessful work or to gloss
over an embarrassing situation. The Preface to *All for Love* be-
longs to this second category.

Much of the Preface appears disingenuous. Far from having
"excelled myself" in *All for Love* (perhaps with reference to
earlier heroic dramas such as *The Conquest of Granada*), Dryden
worked at cross-purposes. Neither the play nor its subtitle bears
out his contention that he was attracted to the story of Antony
and Cleopatra by "the excellency of the moral" the Preface claims
to find there, the punishment of "unlawful love." The difficulty
with the confrontation between Octavia and Cleopatra in Alexandria is not, as Dryden must have realized, that it divides the
audience's sympathies, or that it is unhistorical, but that it makes
Octavia look like an overly aggressive middle-class housewife
invading her unfaithful husband's "love nest." Can Dryden
really have preferred the exchange in Act I between Antony and

Ventidius, after which Antony retains little tragic stature, "to anything which I have written in this kind"—and what "kind" is it, beyond a faint "imitation" of Shakespeare's quarrel scene between Brutus and Cassius (*Julius Caesar*, IV.iii)? A sequence of neatly dovetailed *non sequiturs*, the Preface is primarily Dryden's long-delayed attempt to smother the attack on him in *An Allusion to Horace, the Tenth Satyr of the First Book*, which had been circulating in manuscript since its composition during the winter of 1675–1676 by the witty young courtier John Wilmot, second Earl of Rochester (1647–1680).

Originally Dryden and Rochester were friendly. In the spring of 1673, Dryden had dedicated *Marriage a la Mode* to the Earl and had written him an obsequious letter. By late 1675, however, he accepted as patron Rochester's enemy the Earl of Mulgrave, to whom he dedicated *Aureng-Zebe*, his last new play to be produced before *All for Love*. Concurrently, Thomas Shadwell, with whom Dryden had been quarreling since 1668 and whom Rochester had ridiculed in poems written up to May of 1675, receives high praise in *An Allusion to Horace*. The opening lines of Rochester's satire illustrate its irritating blend of censure with approval:

> Well, sir, 'tis granted I said Dryden's rhymes
> Were stol'n, unequal, nay dull many times.
> What foolish patron is there found of his
> So blindly partial to deny me this?
> But that his plays, embroidered up and down
> With wit and learning, justly pleased the town
> In the same paper I as freely own.
> Yet having this allowed, the heavy mass
> That stuffs up his loose volumes must not pass . . .[41]

Shortly afterward, Shadwell apparently precipitated *Mac Flecknoe* by attacking Dryden in his comedy *The Virtuoso*, acted in May and published early in July of 1676. Shadwell's "northern dedication" to the Duke of Newcastle, in particular, classifies Dryden among "men of feminine understandings" and assails him

[41] *The Complete Poems of John Wilmot, Earl of Rochester*, ed. David M. Vieth (New Haven, 1968), pp. 120–121.

for preferring repartee in comedy, for not liking or understanding "true humor," for allegedly condemning all of Ben Jonson's plays, for his own inferior comedies, and for his pension as Poet Laureate.[42] Dryden took separate revenges on his two antagonists, postponing his retort to the Earl. Meanwhile, literary alliances shifted. Nathaniel Lee, whose *Nero* had been dedicated to Rochester but whose *Sophonisba* is damned in *An Allusion to Horace,* supplied commendatory verses for Dryden's *The State of Innocence* early in 1677 and received similar verses from Dryden later in the year for the first edition of *The Rival Queens,* which is dedicated to Mulgrave; its prologue was contributed by another of Rochester's enemies, Sir Carr Scroope. Although Thomas Otway's *Alcibiades* is disparaged in *An Allusion,* his *Don Carlos* was enthusiastically promoted by Rochester during the spring of 1676, and Otway's preface to the printed play is friendly to Shadwell and hostile to Dryden. His *Titus and Berenice* was dedicated to Rochester early in 1677.

In the form Dryden gave his Preface to *All for Love* early in 1678, its clever display of genuine erudition nevertheless verges upon pedantry, while its refusal to credit Rochester with simple literacy is transparently unfair.[43]

THE EPISTLE DEDICATORY

The dedication of *All for Love,* to King Charles's powerful minister the Earl of Danby, is superb English prose, a suave exercise in the art of compliment, and an eloquent early formulation of the political principles Dryden expressed later in *Absalom and Achitophel, The Medal,* and *To My Honor'd Kinsman, John Driden.* Dryden's "eminently constitutional Toryism"[44] abhors

---

[42] *The Virtuoso,* ed. Marjorie Hope Nicolson and David Stuart Rodes (Lincoln, Nebr., 1966), pp. 4–5, where Shadwell's allusions to Dryden are not explained.

[43] For a more favorable estimate of Dryden's Preface, see Frank Livingstone Huntley, "Dryden, Rochester, and the Eighth Satire of Juvenal," *Philological Quarterly,* XVIII (1939), 269–284.

[44] A phrase adapted from Louis I. Bredvold by Nicholas Joost, "Dryden's *Medal* and the Baroque in Politics and the Arts," *Modern Age,* III (1959), 148–155.

the republican tendencies of Shaftesbury and his followers but also, in its insistence upon the rule of law, rejects the "divine right" doctrine and the absolutist views of Hobbes and Filmer. Avoiding equally the extremes of "arbitrary power of one in a monarchy" and "of many in a commonwealth," it supports the existing English "government which has all the advantages of liberty beyond a commonwealth, and all the marks of kingly sovereignty without the danger of a tyranny." Typically astute is Dryden's warning against a tyranny of the majority.

Although Dryden's decision to address *All for Love* to Danby was thought out well in advance,[45] his dedication may seem unconnected with the play. His statement of political theory, however, activates in the volume as published in 1678 a succession of images of ideal or unsatisfactory monarchs which imposes at least a specious unity. Developing the antithesis between public and private life, as does the dedication, the play calls Antony "emperor" often enough to question his right to the title and ask implicitly what constitutes the ideal ruler. Antony's abundance of talents cannot be integrated to achieve practical control of the Roman world; Octavius, by contrast, possesses the desired efficiency but has few other kingly qualities. Dryden may not have intended any contemporary allusions, but Restoration theatergoers could be forgiven if they visualized Antony as the philandering Charles II, Cleopatra as a politically powerful foreign mistress like the French Duchess of Portsmouth, and Octavius as the all-conquering but personally unsoldier-like Louis XIV.

Prologue and epilogue translate the subject-monarch relationship into the contemporary give-and-take between playwright and theater audience (including other writers). The prologue metaphorically characterizes the audience in relation to the playwright as vultures waiting to devour a dying warrior, street bullies, pygmies anxious to cut a man down to their own small size, and biting fleas, with a culminating, idealized vignette of wealthy patrons accepting homely cheer from a poor tenant. In the epilogue, the monarch-like audience becomes "some antiquated

---

[45] Charles E. Ward, *The Life of John Dryden* (Chapel Hill, 1961), pp. 120, 123.

lady" who "only has the wrinkles of a judge."[46] In the Preface, the satirical portrayal of Rochester as oriental despot, pretending "to decide sovereignly concerning poetry," is followed by Dryden's humorously vivid account of ancient Greek and Roman writers terrorized by jealous tyrants who fancied themselves poets. The two poles of the subject-monarch pattern are the satanic Shaftesbury (or Alexas) and God, whose vicegerent is the King and whose infinite justice, Dolabella reminds us in a lyrical passage, is tempered with mercy (IV.537–543).

The present volume owes debts, acknowledged or not, to virtually all my predecessors in the editing of *All for Love*. My colleague Professor William J. Brown offered helpful suggestions concerning the "friendship" theme in Renaissance literature. Among the many libraries which assisted the project, special thanks are due to the staffs of the Morris Library of Southern Illinois University at Carbondale, the University of Illinois Library at Urbana, the Folger Shakespeare Library, the Humanities Research Center at the University of Texas, and the Pierpont Morgan Library.

David M. Vieth

Southern Illinois University at Carbondale

---

[46] This prologue and epilogue are analyzed in Arthur W. Hoffman, *John Dryden's Imagery* (Gainesville, Fla., 1962), pp. 32–34, 44–46.

ALL FOR LOVE

Facile est verbum aliquod ardens, ut ita dicam, notare idque restinctis animorum incendiis irridere.

—Cicero.

Facile . . . irridere] "It is easy to criticize some passionate word, if I may use the expression, and to laugh at it when the fires in the mind are cooled" (Cicero, *Orator*, VIII). The received text reads *enim verbum* and *iam animorum.*

To the Right Honorable, Thomas Earl of Danby, Viscount Latimer, and Baron Osborne of Kiveton in Yorkshire, Lord High Treasurer of England, One of His Majesty's Most Honorable Privy Council, and Knight of the Most Noble Order of the Garter, etc.

MY LORD,

The gratitude of poets is so troublesome a virtue to great men that you are often in danger of your own benefits; for you are threatened with some epistle, and not suffered to do good in quiet, or to compound for   5
their silence whom you have obliged. Yet I confess I neither am nor ought to be surprised at this indulgence, for your lordship has the same right to favor poetry which the great and noble have ever had.

Carmen amat, quisquis carmine digna gerit.   10

There is somewhat of a tie in nature betwixt those who are born for worthy actions and those who can transmit them to posterity, and though ours be much the inferior part, it comes at least within the verge of alliance; nor are we unprofitable members of the common-   15
wealth when we animate others to those virtues which we copy and describe from you.

Thomas Osborne, first Earl of Danby (1631–1712), was at this time Charles II's principal minister. Basically anti-French and anti-Catholic, he was a firm advocate of royal authority. He was Lord High Treasurer of England from 1673 to 1679, when he was impeached by Parliament and imprisoned in the Tower until 1684. Later he was created Marquess of Carmarthen and Duke of Leeds.

10. *Carmen . . . gerit*] "Everyone loves poetry who does deeds worthy of poetry" (Claudian, XXIII.6).

11–17. *There is . . . from you*] In *To My Honor'd Kinsman, John Driden,* Dryden similarly pairs his cousin with himself: "One to perform, another to record" (l. 204).

'Tis indeed their interest, who endeavor the subversion of governments, to discourage poets and historians, for the best which can happen to them is to be forgotten. 20 But such who, under kings, are the fathers of their country, and by a just and prudent ordering of affairs preserve it, have the same reason to cherish the chroniclers of their actions as they have to lay up in safety the deeds and evidences of their estates: for such records are their 25 undoubted titles to the love and reverence of after ages. Your lordship's administration has already taken up a considerable part of the English annals, and many of its most happy years are owing to it. His Majesty, the most knowing judge of men and the best master, has acknowl- 30 edged the ease and benefit he receives in the incomes of his Treasury, which you found not only disordered but exhausted. All things were in the confusion of a chaos, without form or method, if not reduced beyond it even to annihilation, so that you had not only to separate the 35 jarring elements but (if that boldness of expression might be allowed me) to create them. Your enemies had so embroiled the management of your office that they looked on your advancement as the instrument of your ruin. And as if the clogging of the revenue and the con- 40 fusion of accounts, which you found in your entrance, were not sufficient, they added their own weight of malice to the public calamity by forestalling the credit which should cure it. Your friends on the other side were only capable of pitying, but not of aiding you. No farther 45 help or counsel was remaining to you but what was founded on yourself, and that indeed was your security; for your diligence, your constancy, and your prudence wrought more surely within when they were not dis-

42. added] *Q1–2, C1;* adde *Q3.*

18–20. *'Tis indeed . . . forgotten*] Cf. *Absalom and Achitophel,* Part I, l. 873: "And never rebel was to arts a friend."

33–37. *chaos . . . create them*] With this allusion to the Creation, when the divine Logos was imposed upon Chaos or Nothing, Dryden initiates the theological metaphor that furnishes much of the imaginative framework of his dedication.

turbed by any outward motion. The highest virtue is best 50
to be trusted with itself, for assistance only can be given
by a genius superior to that which it assists. And 'tis
the noblest kind of debt when we are only obliged to
God and nature.

This, then, my lord, is your just commendation, that 55
you have wrought out yourself a way to glory by those
very means that were designed for your destruction. You
have not only restored but advanced the revenues of your
Master without grievance to the subject; and as if that
were little yet, the debts of the Exchequer, which lay 60
heaviest both on the Crown and on private persons, have
by your conduct been established in a certainty of satisfac-
tion—an action so much the more great and honorable
because the case was without the ordinary relief of laws,
above the hopes of the afflicted, and beyond the narrow- 65
ness of the Treasury to redress, had it been managed
by a less able hand. 'Tis certainly the happiest and most
unenvied part of all your fortune to do good to many
while you do injury to none: to receive at once the
prayers of the subject and the praises of the prince, and 70
by the care of your conduct, to give him means of ex-
erting the chiefest (if any be the chiefest) of his royal
virtues, his distributive justice to the deserving and his
bounty and compassion to the wanting.

The disposition of princes towards their people cannot 75
better be discovered than in the choice of their ministers,
who, like the animal spirits betwixt the soul and body,

---

51. itself] it self *Q1,C1;* its self
Q2–3.

---

60. *debts of the Exchequer*] Public panic ensued when, in January,
1671/2, a shortage of the funds needed to carry on the war against the
Dutch caused King Charles to suspend all payments on debts owed
by the government to private bankers. Lord Clifford, who recom-
mended the measure, was made Lord High Treasurer, in which office
he was succeeded in 1673 by Osborne.

77. *animal spirits*] The highest of three "spirits" in the blood, the
animal spirits were thought to provide an essential linkage between
man's mental and physical processes.

participate somewhat of both natures, and make the communication which is betwixt them. A king who is just and moderate in his nature, who rules according to the 80 laws, whom God made happy by forming the temper of his soul to the constitution of his government, and who makes us happy by assuming over us no other sovereignty than that wherein our welfare and liberty consists—a prince, I say, of so excellent a character, and so suitable 85 to the wishes of all good men, could not better have conveyed himself into his people's apprehensions than in your lordship's person, who so lively express the same virtues that you seem not so much a copy as an emanation of him. Moderation is doubtless an establishment of 90 greatness, but there is a steadiness of temper which is likewise requisite in a minister of state: so equal a mixture of both virtues that he may stand like an isthmus betwixt the two encroaching seas of arbitrary power and lawless anarchy. The undertaking would be difficult to 95 any but an extraordinary genius, to stand at the line and to divide the limits; to pay what is due to the great representative of the nation, and neither to enhance nor to yield up the undoubted prerogatives of the Crown.

These, my lord, are the proper virtues of a noble 100 Englishman, as indeed they are properly English virtues, no people in the world being capable of using them but we who have the happiness to be born under so equal and so well-poised a government—a government which has all the advantages of liberty beyond a commonwealth, 105 and all the marks of kingly sovereignty without the dan-

---

92–99. *so equal . . . Crown*] Cf. *To My Honor'd Kinsman, John Driden,* ll. 171 ff.: "A patriot both the King and country serves;/ Prerogative and privilege preserves:/ Of each, our laws the certain limit show;/ One must not ebb, nor t'other overflow./ Betwixt the prince and Parliament we stand,/ The barriers of the state on either hand;/ May neither overflow, for then they drown the land." Dryden described this poem as "my Own opinion, of what an Englishman in Parliament oughto be . . . a Memorial of my own Principles to all Posterity" (*The Letters of John Dryden,* ed. Charles E. Ward, Durham, N. C., 1942, p. 120).

ger of a tyranny. Both my nature, as I am an Englishman, and my reason, as I am a man, have bred in me a
loathing to that specious name of a republic: that mock
appearance of a liberty, where all who have not part in 110
the government are slaves, and slaves they are of a viler
note than such as are subjects to an absolute dominion.
For no Christian monarchy is so absolute but 'tis cir-
cumscribed with laws; but when the executive power is in
the lawmakers, there is no farther check upon them, 115
and the people must suffer without a remedy because
they are oppressed by their representatives. If I must
serve, the number of my masters, who were born my
equals, would but add to the ignominy of my bondage.
The nature of our government, above all others, is 120
exactly suited both to the situation of our country and
the temper of the natives, an island being more proper
for commerce and for defense than for extending its
dominions on the Continent; for what the valor of its
inhabitants might gain, by reason of its remoteness and 125
the casualties of the seas it could not so easily preserve.
And therefore neither the arbitrary power of one in
a monarchy, nor of many in a commonwealth, could
make us greater than we are. 'Tis true that vaster and
more frequent taxes might be gathered when the consent 130
of the people was not asked or needed, but this were only
by conquering abroad to be poor at home; and the examples of our neighbors teach us that they are not always
the happiest subjects whose kings extend their dominions
farthest.   135
    Since, therefore, we cannot win by an offensive war,
at least a land war, the model of our government seems
naturally contrived for the defensive part, and the consent of a people is easily obtained to contribute to that

120. others] *Q1–2;* other *Q3,C1.*

133. *our neighbors*] Now at the height of his military successes,
Louis XIV was about to complete a victorious war against the Dutch
(from which the English had withdrawn in 1674) with the Treaties of
Nimeguen, 1678–1679.

power which must protect it. *Felices nimium, bona si* 140
sua nórint, Angligenae! And yet there are not wanting
malcontents amongst us who, surfeiting themselves on
too much happiness, would persuade the people that
they might be happier by a change. 'Twas indeed the
policy of their old forefather, when himself was fallen 145
from the station of glory, to seduce mankind into the
same rebellion with him by telling him he might yet be
freer than he was; that is, more free than his nature
would allow, or (if I may so say) than God could make
him. We have already all the liberty which freeborn 150
subjects can enjoy, and all beyond it is but license.
But if it be liberty of conscience which they pretend,
the moderation of our church is such that its practice
extends not to the severity of persecution, and its dis-
cipline is withal so easy that it allows more freedom to 155
dissenters than any of the sects would allow to it. In the
meantime, what right can be pretended by these men to
attempt innovations in church or state? Who made them
the trustees or (to speak a little nearer their own
language) the keepers of the liberty of England? If their 160

142. amongst] *Q1–3;* among *C1.*

140–141. *Felices . . . Angligenae*] "Happy Englishmen! too happy,
should they come to know their blessings!" This is adapted from the
opening lines of Virgil's "happy husbandman" passage *(Georgics*
II.458–459), a *locus classicus* of the tradition of "retirement" which
is also reflected in Antony's retreat from the world in Act I.

141–151. *And yet . . . license*] Cf. *Absalom and Achitophel*, Part I,
ll. 45–56, e.g., ll. 51–52: "These Adam-wits, too fortunately free,/
Began to dream they wanted liberty."

145. *their old forefather*] the arch-rebel Satan, to whom Anthony
Ashley Cooper, first Earl of Shaftesbury, was to be compared in
Absalom and Achitophel and *The Medal.*

152. *liberty of conscience*] a slogan of the Puritans, Shaftesbury's
principal supporters.

160. *keepers*] Dryden's comedy *The Kind Keeper, or Mr. Limberham,* to which Charles II contributed some hints, was acted at the
Duke's House on March 11, 1677/8, a few days before the publication
of *All for Love.* Dryden's "keeper" (in a sexual sense) may be a
satirical caricature of Shaftesbury, and the play's suppression after
three performances may have been due to Shaftesbury's faction.

call be extraordinary, let them convince us by working
miracles; for ordinary vocation they can have none to
disturb the government under which they were born,
and which protects them. He who has often changed
his party, and always has made his interest the rule of 165
it, gives little evidence of his sincerity for the public
good: 'tis manifest he changes but for himself, and takes
the people for tools to work his fortune. Yet the experience of all ages might let him know that they who
trouble the waters first have seldom the benefit of the 170
fishing; as they who began the late rebellion enjoyed not
the fruit of their undertaking, but were crushed themselves by the usurpation of their own instrument. Neither
is it enough for them to answer that they only intend a
reformation of the government, but not the subversion 175
of it. On such pretenses all insurrections have been
founded: 'tis striking at the root of power, which is
obedience. Every remonstrance of private men has the
seed of treason in it, and discourses which are couched
in ambiguous terms are therefore the more dangerous 180
because they do all the mischief of open sedition, yet
are safe from the punishment of the laws.

　These, my lord, are considerations which I should not
pass so lightly over had I room to manage them as they
deserve; for no man can be so inconsiderable in a nation 185
as not to have a share in the welfare of it, and if he be
a true Englishman, he must at the same time be fired
with indignation, and revenge himself as he can on the

180. terms are] *Q2–3,C1*; terms　187. Englishman] *Q1,Q3,C1*; Eng-
ars *Q1*.　　　　　　　　　　　　lishmen *Q2*.

---

　161. *call*] religious duty or vocation regarded as divinely inspired.
　164–165. *He who . . . party*] In his youth, during the Civil War,
Shaftesbury first fought for Charles I but then joined the Parliamentary
side and became an adviser to Cromwell. After supporting the Restoration in 1660 and holding important posts in Charles II's goverment, he
became in 1673 the leader of the party opposing the King. Cf. the
similar account of his career in *The Medal*, ll. 22–81.
　173. *their own instrument*] In 1653 Cromwell dispersed Parliament
and thereafter ruled alone as Lord Protector.

disturbers of his country. And to whom could I more
fitly apply myself than to your lordship, who have not 190
only an inborn but an hereditary loyalty? The memorable constancy and sufferings of your father, almost to
the ruin of his estate for the royal cause, were an earnest
of that which such a parent and such an institution
would produce in the person of a son. But so unhappy 195
an occasion of manifesting your own zeal in suffering for
his present Majesty, the Providence of God and the prudence of your administration will, I hope, prevent; that
as your father's fortune waited on the unhappiness of
his sovereign, so your own may participate of the better 200
fate which attends his son. The relation which you
have by alliance to the noble family of your lady serves
to confirm to you both this happy augury. For what can
deserve a greater place in the English chronicle than the
loyalty and courage, the actions and death, of the general 205
of an army fighting for his prince and country? The
honor and gallantry of the Earl of Lindsey is so illustrious a subject that 'tis fit to adorn an heroic poem, for
he was the protomartyr of the cause, and the type of his
unfortunate royal master.   210
Yet, after all, my lord, if I may speak my thoughts,

---

192. *your father*] Sir Edward Osborne (1596–1647) had been Deputy-
Lieutenant-General of the royalist forces raised at York.

207. *Earl of Lindsey*] Robert Bertie, first Earl of Lindsey (1582–
1642), general-in-chief of the King's forces at the outbreak of the
Civil War, was mortally wounded at the battle of Edgehill, where he
was in command. His son Montagu Bertie, the second Earl (1608?–1666),
who also served loyally in the Civil War, was the father of Danby's
wife Bridget.

209. *protomartyr*] especially Saint Stephen, the first Christian
martyr.

209. *type*] According to the theory of biblical typology in its
narrowest sense, certain persons, things, and events of the Old Testament ("types") are symbolic prefigurations of certain persons, things,
and events of the New Testament ("antitypes"). Thus Moses striking
water from the dry rock is a type of Christ the Redeemer. Cf. *Mac
Flecknoe*, ll. 29–30: "Heywood and Shirley were but types of thee,/
Thou last great prophet of tautology."

you are happy rather to us than to yourself; for the
multiplicity, the cares, and the vexations of your employment have betrayed you from yourself, and given
you up into the possession of the public. You are robbed 215
of your privacy and friends, and scarce any hour of your
life you can call your own. Those who envy your fortune,
if they wanted not good nature, might more justly pity
it; and when they see you watched by a crowd of suitors,
whose importunity 'tis impossible to avoid, would con- 220
clude with reason that you have lost much more in true
content than you have gained by dignity, and that a private gentleman is better attended by a single servant
than your lordship with so clamorous a train. Pardon
me, my lord, if I speak like a philosopher on this 225
subject. The fortune which makes a man uneasy cannot
make him happy, and a wise man must think himself
uneasy when few of his actions are in his choice.

This last consideration has brought me to another,
and a very seasonable one for your relief, which is, that 230
while I pity your want of leisure, I have impertinently
detained you so long a time. I have put off my own
business, which was my dedication, till 'tis so late that
I am now ashamed to begin it. And therefore I will
say nothing of the poem which I present to you, because 235
I know not if you are like to have an hour which, with
a good conscience, you may throw away in perusing it.
And for the author, I have only to beg the continuance
of your protection to him, who is,

My lord,   240

Your lordship's most obliged,

most humble, and most

obedient servant,

JOHN DRYDEN

Preface

The death of Antony and Cleopatra is a subject
which has been treated by the greatest wits of our nation,
after Shakespeare; and by all so variously that their example has given me the confidence to try myself in
this bow of Ulysses amongst the crowd of suitors; and,   5
withal, to take my own measures in aiming at the mark.
I doubt not but the same motive has prevailed with all
of us in this attempt; I mean the excellency of the
moral: for the chief persons represented were famous
patterns of unlawful love, and their end accordingly   10
was unfortunate. All reasonable men have long since concluded that the hero of the poem ought not to be a
character of perfect virtue, for then he could not, without injustice, be made unhappy; nor yet altogether
wicked, because he could not then be pitied. I have   15
therefore steered the middle course, and have drawn
the character of Antony as favorably as Plutarch,

1. Antony] *normalized throughout
to this spelling, which is adopted
regularly by Q1 in the play.*

2. *greatest wits*] Prominent earlier treatments, besides Shakespeare's,
include Mary, Countess of Pembroke's translation of Garnier's French
play (1592); Samuel Daniel's *The Tragedie of Cleopatra* (1594);
Fletcher's *The False One* (acted ca. 1620); Thomas May's *The Tragedie
of Cleopatra Queen of Aegypt* (acted 1626; pub. 1639); and Sir Charles
Sedley's *Antony and Cleopatra* (acted Feb. 12, 1676/7; pub. 1677).
    5. *bow of Ulysses*] Odyssey, XXI–XXII.
    8–9. *excellency of the moral*] Dryden's moralistic view of tragedy
may have been strengthened by the publication, in midsummer of
1677, of Thomas Rymer's *The Tragedies of the Last Age Consider'd.*
Nevertheless, the concept of "poetical justice," the term invented by
Rymer, was already implicit in Dryden's earlier criticism.
    11–15. *All reasonable . . . pitied*] a dictum of Aristotle, *Poetics,*
XIII.
    17. *as favorably as*] "But my characters of Anthony and Cleopatra,
though they are favorable to them, have nothing of outrageous
panegyric. Their passions were their own, and such as were given
them by history; only the deformities of them were cast into shadows,

Appian, and Dion Cassius would give me leave; the
like I have observed in Cleopatra. That which is wanting
to work up the pity to a greater height was not afforded   20
me by the story: for the crimes of love which they both
committed were not occasioned by any necessity, or fatal
ignorance, but were wholly voluntary; since our passions
are, or ought to be, within our power.

The fabric of the play is regular enough, as to the   25
inferior parts of it; and the unities of time, place, and
action more exactly observed than, perhaps, the English
theater requires. Particularly, the action is so much one
that it is the only of the kind without episode or underplot; every scene in the tragedy conducing to the main   30
design, and every act concluding with a turn of it. The
greatest error in the contrivance seems to be in the person of Octavia; for, though I might use the privilege of a
poet to introduce her into Alexandria, yet I had not
enough considered that the compassion she moved to   35
herself and children was destructive to that which I
reserved for Antony and Cleopatra; whose mutual love,
being founded upon vice, must lessen the favor of the
audience to them, when virtue and innocence were oppressed by it. And though I justified Antony in some   40
measure by making Octavia's departure to proceed
wholly from herself, yet the force of the first machine
still remained; and the dividing of pity, like the cutting

---

that they might be objects of compassion; whereas if I had chosen a
noonday light for them, somewhat must have been discovered which
would rather have moved our hatred than our pity" (Dryden, *A
Parallel betwixt Painting and Poetry*, 1695).
    17–18. *Plutarch, Appian, and Dion Cassius*] Plutarch's *Life of
Marcus Antonius* in North's translation is the major source of Shakespeare's play, which in turn is the major source of Dryden's. Appian
and Dio Cassius each wrote histories of Rome in the Greek language
which survive only in part.
    22–23. *necessity, or fatal ignorance*] regarded by Rymer as condi-
tions requisite for a truly tragic protagonist.
    31. *turn*] change in the state of affairs.
    42. *machine*] contrivance.

of a river into many channels, abated the strength of
the natural stream.   45
    But this is an objection which none of my critics
have urged against me, and therefore I might have let
it pass, if I could have resolved to have been partial
to myself. The faults my enemies have found are rather
cavils concerning little, and not essential decencies;   50
which a master of the ceremonies may decide betwixt
us. The French poets, I confess, are strict observers of
these punctilios. They would not, for example, have
suffered Cleopatra and Octavia to have met; or, if they
had met, there must only have passed betwixt them   55
some cold civilities, but no eagerness of repartee, for
fear of offending against the greatness of their characters
and the modesty of their sex. This objection I foresaw,
and at the same time contemned; for I judged it both
natural and probable that Octavia, proud of her new-   60
gained conquest, would search out Cleopatra to triumph
over her, and that Cleopatra, thus attacked, was not of
a spirit to shun the encounter. And 'tis not unlikely
that two exasperated rivals should use such satire as
I have put into their mouths; for, after all, though the 65
one were a Roman and the other a queen, they were
both women. 'Tis true, some actions, though natural, are
not fit to be represented, and broad obscenities in words
ought in good manners to be avoided; expressions therefore are a modest clothing of our thoughts, as breeches   70
and petticoats are of our bodies. If I have kept myself
within the bounds of modesty, all beyond it is but nicety
and affectation, which is no more but modesty depraved
into a vice. They betray themselves who are too quick
of apprehension in such cases, and leave all reason-   75
able men to imagine worse of them than of the poet.
    Honest Montaigne goes yet farther: *Nous ne sommes
que cérémonie; la cérémonie nous emporte, et laissons*

77–88. *Nous . . . croit*] "We are nothing but ceremony; ceremony
carries us away, and we leave the substance of things. We hold on to
the branches and abandon the trunk and the body. We have taught

la substance des choses. Nous nous tenons aux branches,
et abandonnons le tronc et le corps. Nous avons appris   80
aux dames de rougir, oyans seulement nommer ce
qu'elles ne craignent aucunement à faire: nous n'osons
appeller à droit nos membres, et ne craignons pas de les
employer à toute sorte de débauche. La cérémonie nous
défend d'exprimer par paroles les choses licites et   85
naturelles, et nous l'en croyons; la raison nous défend
de n'en faire point d'illicites et mauvaises, et personne
ne l'en croit. My comfort is that by this opinion, my
enemies are but sucking critics, who would fain be
nibbling ere their teeth are come.   90

Yet in this nicety of manners does the excellency of
French poetry consist: their heroes are the most civil
people breathing, but their good breeding seldom extends to a word of sense. All their wit is in their ceremony; they want the genius which animates our stage;   95
and therefore 'tis but necessary, when they cannot please,
that they should take care not to offend. But as the
civilest man in the company is commonly the dullest,
so these authors, while they are afraid to make you laugh

80. *tronc*] *Q1–3; trone C1.*   83. *pas*] *Q1; par Q2–3,C1.*
82. *n'osons*] *Q1–2; n'esons Q3,C1.*   88. *croit*] *croid Q1–2,C1; eroid Q3.*

---

the ladies to blush at merely hearing named what they are not at all
afraid to do: we dare not call our members by their right names, yet
we are not afraid to employ them in all sorts of debauchery. Ceremony forbids us to express in words things that are permissible and
natural, and we obey it; reason forbids us to do things illicit and
wicked, and nobody obeys it" *(Essais,* II, 17). Somewhat irrelevant in
Dryden's context, the quotation thematically resembles *The Plain
Dealer* by his friend William Wycherley, acted on December 11, 1676,
and praised highly in Dryden's "Apology for Heroic Poetry and
Poetic Licence" prefixed to *The State of Innocence* early in 1677.
Wycherley's famous mock dedication to "Lady" Bennet draws repeatedly upon "the plain dealer Montaigne."

89. *sucking critics*] In *An Allusion to Horace,* the Earl of Rochester
amusingly parallels himself with Horace and Dryden with Lucilius, a
relatively crude poet of several generations earlier. Dryden, who was
sixteen years older than Rochester, apparently reverses the insult by
calling him an infant.

or cry, out of pure good manners make you sleep. They 100
are so careful not to exasperate a critic that they never
leave him any work; so busy with the broom, and make
so clean a riddance, that there is little left either for
censure or for praise. For no part of a poem is worth
our discommending where the whole is insipid; as when 105
we have once tasted of palled wine, we stay not to ex-
amine it glass by glass.

But while they affect to shine in trifles, they are often
careless in essentials. Thus their Hippolytus is so scrup-
ulous in point of decency that he will rather expose him- 110
self to death than accuse his stepmother to his father;
and my critics, I am sure, will commend him for it. But
we of grosser apprehensions are apt to think that this
excess of generosity is not practicable but with fools
and madmen. This was good manners with a vengeance, 115
and the audience is like to be much concerned at the
misfortunes of this admirable hero. But take Hippolytus
out of his poetic fit, and I suppose he would think it a
wiser part to set the saddle on the right horse, and choose
rather to live with the reputation of a plain-spoken, hon- 120
est man, than to die with the infamy of an incestuous
villain. In the meantime we may take notice that where
the poet ought to have preserved the character as it was
delivered to us by antiquity, when he should have given
us the picture of a rough young man of the Amazonian 125
strain, a jolly huntsman, and both by his profession
and his early rising a mortal enemy to love, he has chosen

108. trifles] *Q1,Q3,C1;* ttifles *Q2.*

---

106. *palled*] stale.
109. *their Hippolytus*] in Racine's tragedy *Phèdre,* produced on
January 1, 1677 (New Style), and published later that year. Dryden's
ungenerous strictures on Racine's masterpiece may have been promp-
ted by a flurry of English plays adapted from the French during the
season of 1676–1677, notably Thomas Otway's successful *Titus and
Berenice,* which was translated from Racine's *Bérénice* and dedicated
to Otway's patron, the Earl of Rochester. This play probably influ-
enced *All for Love,* especially Dryden's treatment of his "emperor,"
"friend," and "mistress" in Act IV.

to give him the turn of gallantry, sent him to travel
from Athens to Paris, taught him to make love, and
transformed the Hippolytus of Euripides into Monsieur   130
Hippolyte.

I should not have troubled myself thus far with
French poets, but that I find our *Chedreux* critics wholly
form their judgments by them. But for my part, I desire
to be tried by the laws of my own country; for it seems   135
unjust to me that the French should prescribe here till
they have conquered. Our little sonneteers who follow
them have too narrow souls to judge of poetry. Poets
themselves are the most proper, though I conclude not
the only, critics. But till some genius as universal as   140
Aristotle shall arise, one who can penetrate into all arts
and sciences without the practice of them, I shall think
it reasonable that the judgment of an artificer in his own
art should be preferable to the opinion of another man,
at least where he is not bribed by interest or prejudiced 145
by malice. And this, I suppose, is manifest by plain
induction. For, first, the crowd cannot be presumed to
have more than a gross instinct of what pleases or dis-
pleases them. Every man will grant me this; but then,
by a particular kindness to himself, he draws his own   150
stake first, and will be distinguished from the multitude,
of which other men may think him one.

But if I come closer to those who are allowed for
witty men, either by the advantage of their quality or by
common fame, and affirm that neither are they qualified 155
to decide sovereignly concerning poetry, I shall yet
have a strong party of my opinion; for most of them
severally will exclude the rest, either from the number

141. one who] *Q1;* who *Q2–3,C1.*   145. where] *Q1–2,C1;* there *Q3.*

---

130. *the Hippolytus of Euripides*] Euripides's *Hippolytus,* Racine's
principal source, receives special praise from Rymer.

133. *Chedreux*] a fashionable wig-maker of the day.

150–151. *draws his own stake*] withdraws his own wager.

153–315. *But if . . . considering him*] This long passage is a con-
tinuous attack on the Earl of Rochester.

of witty men, or at least of able judges. But here again
they are all indulgent to themselves; and everyone who 160
believes himself a wit, that is, every man, will pretend
at the same time to a right of judging. But to press it
yet farther, there are many witty men, but few poets;
neither have all poets a taste of tragedy. And this is the
rock on which they are daily splitting. Poetry, which is 165
a picture of nature, must generally please; but 'tis not
to be understood that all parts of it must please every
man; therefore is not tragedy to be judged by a witty
man whose taste is only confined to comedy. Nor is every
man who loves tragedy a sufficient judge of it: he must 170
understand the excellencies of it too, or he will only
prove a blind admirer, not a critic. From hence it comes
that so many satires on poets, and censures of their
writings, fly abroad. Men of pleasant conversation (at
least esteemed so), and indued with a trifling kind of 175
fancy, perhaps helped out with some smattering of
Latin, are ambitious to distinguish themselves from the
herd of gentlemen by their poetry—

> *Rarus enim fermè sensus communis in illâ*
> *Fortunâ.* 180

And is not this a wretched affectation, not to be
contented with what fortune has done for them, and
sit down quietly with their estates, but they must call

167. to be understood] *Q1,Q3,C1;*
be understood *Q2.*

173-174. *satires . . . fly abroad] An Allusion to Horace,* one of several verse attacks on Dryden about this date, circulated widely in manuscript before its first publication in 1680. Contrary to the innuendo
later in Dryden's Preface, Rochester's authorship of the poem was no
secret.

178. *herd of gentlemen]* Cf. Pope's "mob of gentlemen who wrote
with ease" *(Epistle to Augustus,* l. 108)—referring, of course, to
Rochester and similar "wits of either Charles's days."

179-180. *Rarus . . . Fortunâ]* "For common sense is rare in that
station of life" (Juvenal, *Satires* VIII.73-74).

their wits in question, and needlessly expose their
nakedness to public view? not considering that they are 185
not to expect the same approbation from sober men
which they have found from their flatterers after the
third bottle. If a little glittering in discourse has passed
them on us for witty men, where was the necessity of
undeceiving the world? Would a man who has an ill 190
title to an estate, but yet is in possession of it, would
he bring it of his own accord to be tried at Westminster?
We who write, if we want the talent, yet have the excuse
that we do it for a poor subsistence; but what can be
urged in their defense who, not having the vocation of 195
poverty to scribble, out of mere wantonness take pains
to make themselves ridiculous? Horace was certainly in
the right where he said that "no man is satisfied with
his own condition." A poet is not pleased because he
is not rich; and the rich are discontented because the 200
poets will not admit them of their number. Thus the
case is hard with writers: if they succeed not, they must
starve; and if they do, some malicious satire is prepared
to level them for daring to please without their leave.
But while they are so eager to destroy the fame of others, 205
their ambition is manifest in their concernment: some
poem of their own is to be produced, and the slaves are
to be laid flat with their faces on the ground, that the
monarch may appear in the greater majesty.

184–185. *expose their nakedness*] possibly glancing at rumors during September and October of 1677 that Rochester was running about
stark naked with his guests in Woodstock Park, of which he was Ranger
and Keeper.

197. *Horace*] in *Satires* I.i.1–3.

207–209. *slaves . . . majesty*] Dedicating his comedy *Marriage
à la Mode* to Rochester in 1673 while the two men were still on good
terms, Dryden ranked himself "amongst your slaves" and concluded
prophetically, "Your lordship has but another step to make, and
from the patron of wit, you may become its tyrant, and oppress our
little reputations with more ease than you now protect them."

Dionysius and Nero had the same longings, but with 210
all their power they could never bring their business
well about. 'Tis true, they proclaimed themselves poets
by sound of trumpet; and poets they were, upon pain of
death to any man who durst call them otherwise. The
audience had a fine time on't, you may imagine. They 215
sat in a bodily fear, and looked as demurely as they
could, for 'twas a hanging matter to laugh unseasonably,
and the tyrants were suspicious, as they had reason, that
their subjects had 'em in the wind: so every man, in
his own defense, set as good a face upon the business 220
as he could. 'Twas known beforehand that the monarchs
were to be crowned laureates; but when the show was
over, and an honest man was suffered to depart quietly,
he took out his laughter which he had stifled, with a firm
resolution never more to see an emperor's play, though 225
he had been ten years a-making it. In the meantime, the
true poets were they who made the best markets, for
they had wit enough to yield the prize with a good grace,
and not contend with him who had thirty legions. They
were sure to be rewarded if they confessed themselves 230
bad writers, and that was somewhat better than to be
martyrs for their reputation. Lucan's example was
enough to teach them manners; and after he was put

---

210. *Dionysius and Nero*] Both Dionysius, tyrant of Syracuse, and
the Roman emperor Nero nursed literary ambitions and were insanely
jealous of competitors. In 367 B.C. Dionysius's tragedy *The Ransom of
Hector* was awarded the first prize at Athens as a political expedient.

226. *ten years a-making it*] Horace's celebrated advice was to polish
one's poem for *nine* years *(Ars Poetica,* ll. 388–389).

229. *thirty legions*] A philosopher, reproached for disputing very
weakly with the Emperor Hadrian, answered, "Why, would you have
me contend with him that commands thirty legions?" (Bacon,
Apophthegms; derived from Spartianus's *Life of Hadrian,* XIV, this
anecdote is also retold by Montaigne, *Essais,* III, vii).

232. *Lucan's example*] When Nero, who also aspired to literary
eminence, forbade him to recite his poetry in public, Lucan joined
the conspiracy of Piso in A.D. 65. Nero ordered him to commit suicide,
which he did by submitting to have his veins opened, meanwhile re-
peating some of his own verses.

to death for overcoming Nero, the emperor carried it
without dispute for the best poet in his dominions. No 235
man was ambitious of that grinning honor, for if he
heard the malicious trumpeter proclaiming his name
before his betters, he knew there was but one way with
him.

Maecenas took another course, and we know he was 240
more than a great man, for he was witty too; but finding
himself far gone in poetry, which Seneca assures us
was not his talent, he thought it his best way to be well
with Virgil and with Horace, that at least he might be
a poet at the second hand; and we see how happily it has 245
succeeded with him, for his own bad poetry is forgotten,
and their panegyrics of him still remain. But they who
should be our patrons are for no such expensive ways
to fame: they have much of the poetry of Maecenas, but
little of his liberality. They are for persecuting Horace 250
and Virgil in the persons of their successors (for such is
every man who has any part of their soul and fire, though
in a less degree). Some of their little zanies yet go farther,
for they are persecutors even of Horace himself, as far
as they are able, by their ignorant and vile imitations 255

250–251. persecuting . . . Virgil]   253. farther] *Q1–3;* further *C1.*
Q1–3; procuring themselves repu-
tation *C1.*

---

236. *grinning honor*] Falstaff's phrase for the dead Sir Walter
Blunt in *1 Henry IV*, V.iii. The end of Dryden's sentence, "he knew
there was but one way with him," echoes the death of Falstaff in another play about kingship, *Henry V*, II.iii.

242. *Seneca assures us*] See his *Epistolae Morales* XIX.9, XCII.35,
CI.11, CXIV.4–6.

253. *zanies*] A zany is a comic performer attending on a clown,
acrobat, or mountebank, who imitates his master's acts in a ludicrously
awkward way. In the anonymous *A Session of the Poets* written about
November of 1676, Rochester's protégé Thomas Otway is called "Tom
Shadwell's dear zany." Dryden may actually allude to the episode in
which Rochester, probably in 1675 or 1676, masqueraded as the
quack doctor Alexander Bendo, setting up practice on Tower Hill
and issuing a mock mountebank bill that has survived in several
texts. Dryden's pretense that Rochester himself did not write *An
Allusion to Horace* is merely a precautionary evasion.

of him—by making an unjust use of his authority, and
turning his artillery against his friends. But how would
he disdain to be copied by such hands! I dare answer
for him, he would be more uneasy in their company
than he was with Crispinus, their forefather, in the 260
Holy Way; and would no more have allowed them a
place amongst the critics than he would Demetrius the
mimic and Tigellius the buffoon:

> Demetri, teque, Tigelli,
> Discipulorum inter jubeo plorare cathedras. 265

With what scorn would he look down on such miserable
translators, who make doggerel of his Latin, mistake his
meaning, misapply his censures, and often contradict
their own! He is fixed as a landmark to set out the
bounds of poetry, 270

> Saxum antiquum, ingens, . . .
> Limes agro positus, litem ut discerneret arvis.

But other arms than theirs, and other sinews, are
required to raise the weight of such an author; and when
they would toss him against their enemies, 275

> Genua labant, gelidus concrevit frigore sanguis.
> Tum lapis ipse viri, vacuum per inane volutus,
> Nec spatium evasit totum neque pertulit ictum.

276. Genua] Q1–3; Cenua C1.

260–261. Crispinus . . . Holy Way] Perhaps following Jonson's The
Poetaster, Dryden here identifies Crispinus, a bad poet ridiculed else-
where in Horace's works, with the bore who collars him in the Via
Sacra in Satires I.ix.

264–265. Demetri . . . cathedras] "Demetrius and you, Tigellius,
I bid go whine among your pupils' easy chairs" (Horace, Satires
I.x.90–91). The accepted reading is discipularum rather than Dryden's
masculine form.

271–272. Saxum . . . arvis] "a huge and ancient stone, . . . placed
as a boundary in a field, to keep litigation away from the plough-
lands" (Aeneid XII.897–898).

276–278. Genua . . . ictum] "His knees totter, his blood has con-
gealed with cold. Then the hero's rock itself, whirled through empty
space, has failed to traverse all the distance or to carry home its
blow" (Aeneid XII.905–907).

For my part, I would wish no other revenge, either
for myself or the rest of the poets, from this rhyming 280
judge of the twelvepenny gallery, this legitimate son of
Sternhold, than that he would subscribe his name to
his censure or (not to tax him beyond his learning) set
his mark. For should he own himself publicly, and
come from behind the lion's skin, they whom he con- 285
demns would be thankful to him, they whom he praises
would choose to be condemned, and the magistrates
whom he has elected would modestly withdraw from
their employment to avoid the scandal of his nomination.
The sharpness of his satire, next to himself, falls most 290
heavily on his friends, and they ought never to forgive
him for commending them perpetually the wrong way,
and sometimes by contraries. If he have a friend whose
hastiness in writing is his greatest fault, Horace would
have taught him to have minced the matter, and to have 295
called it readiness of thought and a flowing fancy; for
friendship will allow a man to christen an imperfection
by the name of some neighbor virtue:

> *Vellem in amicitiâ sic erraremus, et isti*
> *Errori nomen virtus posuisset honestum.*   300

---

281. *twelvepenny gallery*] Located in the upper gallery, the cheapest
seats in the theaters cost one shilling apiece.

282. *Sternhold*] Together with John Hopkins, Thomas Sternhold
produced the sixteenth-century metrical version of the Psalms which
was long used in public worship in English churches. His name became synonymous with bad poetry.

285. *lion's skin*] probably a double allusion to (1) Aesop's fable
of the ass who tries to impress others by disguising himself in a
lion's skin, but is recognized by his braying; (2) a royal "protection,"
technically signifying Rochester's privilege as a peer against arrest in
a civil suit.

287–288. *magistrates . . . elected*] *An Allsion to Horace* concludes:
"I loathe the rabble; 'tis enough for me/ If Sedley, Shadwell, Shep-
herd, Wycherley,/ Godolphin, Butler, Buckhurst, Buckingham,/
And some few more, whom I omit to name,/ Approve my sense: I
count their censure fame."

299–300. *Vellem . . . honestum*] "I could wish that we erred similarly in friendship, and that on such a mistake good sense had be-
stowed an honorable name" (Horace, *Satires* I.iii.41–42).

But he would never have allowed him to have called
a slow man hasty, or a hasty writer a slow drudge, as
Juvenal explains it:

> *Canibus pigris scabieque vetustâ*
> *Levibus et siccae lambentibus ora lucernae*   305
> *Nomen erit pardus tigris leo, si quid adhuc est*
> *Quod fremit in terris violentius.*

Yet Lucretius laughs at a foolish lover even for excusing the imperfections of his mistress:

> *Nigra* μελίχροος *est, immunda et foetida* ἄκοσμος.   310
> *Balba loqui non quit,* τραυλίζει; *muta pudens est, etc.*

But to drive it *ad Aethiopem cygnum* is not to be
endured. I leave him to interpret this by the benefit of
his French version on the other side, and without farther
considering him than I have the rest of my illiterate 315
censors, whom I have disdained to answer because they
are not qualified for judges. It remains that I acquaint
the reader that I have endeavored in this play to follow
the practice of the ancients, who, as Mr. Rymer has

---

302. *slow man . . . slow drudge*] referring to *An Allusion to Horace,*
ll. 41 ff.: "Of all our modern wits, none seems to me/ Once to have
touched upon true comedy/ But hasty Shadwell and slow Wycherley."
Rochester's statement became a cliché of eighteenth-century criticism;
see Pope, *Epistle to Augustus,* l. 85.
304–307. *Canibus . . . violentius*] "Lazy curs, hairless from chronic
mange, who lick the edges of a dry lamp, shall be called 'Panther,'
'Tiger,' 'Lion,' or whatever else roars more furiously in the world"
(Juvenal, *Satires* VIII.34–37).
310–311. *Nigra . . . est, etc.*] "A black girl is 'honey-colored,' one
who is dirty and stinking, 'casual'; if she stammers and cannot con-
verse, 'lisping'; if silent, 'modest'" (Lucretius, *De Rerum Natura*
IV.1160,1164).
312. *ad Aethiopem cygnum*] "to the point of calling an Ethiopian
a swan" (adapted from Juvenal, *Satires* VIII.33). Rochester had set
up shop as a mock-mountebank next door to a tavern called the
Black Swan.
319. *Mr. Rymer*] On rationalistic rather than neoclassical grounds,
Rymer in his *Tragedies of the Last Age* found Greek tragedy superior
to several comparable plays by Beaumont and Fletcher.

judiciously observed, are and ought to be our masters. 320
Horace likewise gives it for a rule in his art of poetry,

> *Vos exemplaria Graeca*
> *Nocturnâ versate manu, versate diurnâ.*

Yet, though their models are regular, they are too
little for English tragedy, which requires to be built in 325
a larger compass. I could give an instance in the *Oedipus
Tyrannus,* which was the masterpiece of Sophocles, but
I reserve it for a more fit occasion, which I hope to have
hereafter. In my style I have professed to imitate the
divine Shakespeare; which that I might perform more 330
freely, I have disencumbered myself from rhyme. Not
that I condemn my former way, but that this is more
proper to my present purpose. I hope I need not to
explain myself, that I have not copied my author ser-
vilely: words and phrases must of necessity receive a 335
change in succeeding ages, but 'tis almost a miracle that
much of his language remains so pure, and that he who
began dramatic poetry amongst us, untaught by any
and, as Ben Jonson tells us, without learning, should by
the force of his own genius perform so much that in a 340
manner he has left no praise for any who come after
him. The occasion is fair, and the subject would be
pleasant to handle the difference of styles betwixt him
and Fletcher, and wherein, and how far they are both
to be imitated. But since I must not be overconfident 345

322–323. *Vos . . . diurnâ*] "Study your Greek models night and day"
(*Ars Poetica,* ll. 268–269).

326–327. *Oedipus Tyrannus*] Dryden collaborated with Nathaniel
Lee on an English *Oedipus,* produced late in 1678 and published in
1679.

339. *as Ben Jonson tells us*] in his verses *To the Memory of My
Beloved Master William Shakespeare,* where Shakespeare is said to
have had "small Latin and less Greek."

342–345. *The occasion . . . imitated*] Stimulated partly by Rymer's
attack on Fletcher in *Tragedies of the Last Age,* Dryden compared the
merits of Shakespeare and Fletcher in his "Grounds of Criticism in
Tragedy" prefixed to *Troilus and Cressida,* 1679.

of my own performance after him, it will be prudence in me to be silent. Yet I hope I may affirm, and without vanity, that by imitating him I have excelled myself throughout the play; and particularly, that I prefer the scene betwixt Antony and Ventidius in the first act to 350 anything which I have written in this kind.

PROLOGUE TO ANTONY AND CLEOPATRA

What flocks of critics hover here today, ⎫
As vultures wait on armies for their prey, ⎬
All gaping for the carcass of a play! ⎭
With croaking notes they bode some dire event,
And follow dying poets by the scent.   5
Ours gives himself for gone; y'have watched your time!
He fights this day unarmed, without his rhyme;
And brings a tale which often has been told,
As sad as Dido's, and almost as old.
His hero, whom you wits his bully call,   10
Bates of his mettle, and scarce rants at all.
He's somewhat lewd, but a well-meaning mind;
Weeps much, fights little, but is wondrous kind;
In short, a pattern and companion fit
For all the keeping tonies of the pit.   15
I could name more: a wife, and mistress too, ⎫
Both (to be plain) too good for most of you; ⎬
The wife well-natured, and the mistress true. ⎭
    Now, poets, if your fame has been his care,
Allow him all the candor you can spare.   20
A brave man scorns to quarrel once a day,
Like hectors in at every petty fray.
Let those find fault whose wit's so very small,
They've need to show that they can think at all.
Errors, like straws, upon the surface flow;   25
He who would search for pearls must dive below.
Fops may have leave to level all they can,
As pygmies would be glad to lop a man.

15. all the] *Q1, C1;* all thee *Q2–3.*

0.1. *Antony and Cleopatra*] The form may imply the extent of Dryden's debt to Shakespeare's play.
7. *rhyme*] After championing the use of rhyme in his heroic plays, Dryden abandons it for blank verse in *All for Love.*
11. *Bates . . . all*] abates the bombast of heroic drama.
15. *tonies*] simpletons, with a play on Antony's name. See also I.373.
22. *hectors*] bullies, street brawlers.

Half-wits are fleas, so little and so light,
We scarce could know they live but that they bite.   30
But as the rich, when tired with daily feasts,
For change become their next poor tenant's guests,
Drink hearty draughts of ale from plain brown bowls,
And snatch the homely rasher from the coals;
So you, retiring from much better cheer,   35
For once may venture to do penance here.
And since that plenteous autumn now is past
Whose grapes and peaches have indulged your taste,
Take in good part, from our poor poet's board,
Such riveled fruits as winter can afford.   40

---

40. *riveled*] wrinkled.

PERSONS REPRESENTED

	By
MARK ANTONY	*Mr. Hart*
VENTIDIUS, his general	*Mr. Mohun*
DOLABELLA, his friend	*Mr. Clark*
ALEXAS, the Queen's eunuch	*Mr. Goodman*
SERAPION, Priest of Isis	*Mr. Griffin*
[MYRIS,] another Priest	*Mr. Coysh*
SERVANTS TO ANTONY, [PRIESTS]	
CLEOPATRA, Queen of Egypt	*Mrs. Boutell*
OCTAVIA, Antony's wife	*Mrs. Corey*
CHARMION } Cleopatra's maids	
IRAS }	
ANTONY'S TWO LITTLE DAUGHTERS	

Scene: *Alexandria*

---

1. By] *Q1–3; om. C1.*

All for Love

or

The World Well Lost

ACT I

Scene, *The Temple of Isis.*
Enter Serapion, Myris, *Priests of Isis.*

SERAPION.

Portents and prodigies are grown so frequent
That they have lost their name. Our fruitful Nile
Flowed ere the wonted season, with a torrent
So unexpected, and so wondrous fierce,
That the wild deluge overtook the haste   5
Ev'n of the hinds that watched it. Men and beasts
Were borne above the tops of trees that grew
On th'utmost margin of the watermark.
Then with so swift an ebb the flood drove backward,
It slipped from underneath the scaly herd: 10
Here monstrous phocae panted on the shore;
Forsaken dolphins there, with their broad tails,
Lay lashing the departing waves; hard by 'em,
Sea-horses flound'ring in the slimy mud
Tossed up their heads, and dashed the ooze about 'em.   15

Enter Alexas *behind them.*

MYRIS.

Avert these omens, heav'n!

Lost] *Q1–3;* Lost. A Tragedy *C1.*

---

11. *phocae*] seals.
14. *Sea-horses*] hippopotami.

SERAPION.

> Last night, between the hours of twelve and one,
> In a lone aisle o'th' temple while I walked,
> A whirlwind rose, that with a violent blast
> Shook all the dome. The doors around me clapt;   20
> The iron wicket, that defends the vault
> Where the long race of Ptolemies is laid,
> Burst open, and disclosed the mighty dead.
> From out each monument, in order placed,
> An armed ghost start up; the boy-king last   25
> Reared his inglorious head. A peal of groans
> Then followed, and a lamentable voice
> Cried, "Egypt is no more!" My blood ran back,
> My shaking knees against each other knocked;
> On the cold pavement down I fell entranced,   30
> And so unfinished left the horrid scene.

ALEXAS *(showing himself)*.

> And dreamed you this? or did invent the story
> To frighten our Egyptian boys withal,
> And train 'em up betimes in fear of priesthood?

SERAPION.

> My lord, I saw you not,   35
> Nor meant my words should reach your ears; but what
> I uttered was most true.

ALEXAS.   A foolish dream,

> Bred from the fumes of indigested feasts
> And holy luxury.

SERAPION.   I know my duty:

> This goes no farther.

19. violent] *Q1–2, C1;* volent *Q3.*   34. 'em] *Q1–3; om. C1.*
25. start] *Q1–3;* starts *C1.*

19–21. *whirlwind . . . wicket*] For the "imitation" here of *The Fae-
rie Queene,* see Richard N. Ringler, "Dryden at the House of Busi-
rane," *English Studies,* XLIV (1968), 224–229.
25. *start*] started (obsolete past tense).
25. *boy-king*] Cleopatra's younger brother Ptolemy XIV, whom in 47
B.C. Julius Caesar appointed joint ruler of Egypt with her, and whom
she was forced to marry although he was only eleven years old. She
allegedly had him poisoned in 44 B.C.

ALEXAS.   'Tis not fit it should;   40
Nor would the times now bear it, were it true.
All southern, from yon hills, the Roman camp
Hangs o'er us black and threat'ning, like a storm
Just breaking on our heads.

SERAPION.
Our faint Egyptians pray for Antony;   45
But in their servile hearts they own Octavius.

MYRIS.
Why then does Antony dream out his hours,
And tempts not fortune for a noble day
Which might redeem what Actium lost?

ALEXAS.
He thinks 'tis past recovery.

SERAPION.   Yet the foe   50
Seems not to press the siege.

ALEXAS.   Oh, there's the wonder.
Maecenas and Agrippa, who can most
With Caesar, are his foes. His wife Octavia,
Driv'n from his house, solicits her revenge;
And Dolabella, who was once his friend,   55
Upon some private grudge now seeks his ruin:
Yet still war seems on either side to sleep.

SERAPION.
'Tis strange that Antony, for some days past,
Has not beheld the face of Cleopatra,
But here in Isis' temple lives retired,   60
And makes his heart a prey to black despair.

40. should] *Q2–3, C1;* shonld *Q1.*

---

49. *Actium*] where Antony was defeated by Octavius in a naval battle
in 31 B.C., the year before the events depicted in Dryden's play. When
Cleopatra fled with her sixty ships, Antony followed.
52. *can*] can accomplish.
53. *His wife Octavia*] Octavius's sister, whom Antony married in 40 B.C.
after the death of his previous wife, Fulvia. The marriage was part of
the agreement at Brundisium under which Octavius was assigned control of the western half of the Roman empire and Antony the eastern
half.

ALEXAS.

 'Tis true; and we much fear he hopes by absence
 To cure his mind of love.

SERAPION.   If he be vanquished
 Or make his peace, Egypt is doomed to be
 A Roman province, and our plenteous harvests   65
 Must then redeem the scarceness of their soil.
 While Antony stood firm, our Alexandria
 Rivaled proud Rome (dominion's other seat),
 And Fortune, striding like a vast Colossus,
 Could fix an equal foot of empire here.   70

ALEXAS.

 Had I my wish, these tyrants of all nature
 Who lord it o'er mankind, should perish, perish,
 Each by the other's sword; but since our will
 Is lamely followed by our pow'r, we must
 Depend on one, with him to rise or fall.   75

SERAPION.

 How stands the queen affected?

ALEXAS.   Oh, she dotes,
 She dotes, Serapion, on this vanquished man,
 And winds herself about his mighty ruins;
 Whom would she yet forsake, yet yield him up,
 This hunted prey, to his pursuer's hands,   80
 She might preserve us all; but 'tis in vain—
 This changes my designs, this blasts my counsels,
 And makes me use all means to keep him here,
 Whom I could wish divided from her arms
 Far as the earth's deep center. Well, you know   85
 The state of things; no more of your ill omens
 And black prognostics; labor to confirm
 The people's hearts.

Enter Ventidius, *talking aside with a* Gentleman *of Antony's.*

62–63. *absence* . . . *love*] one of several commonplaces of "courtly" or chivalric love in this play. See also IV.74 ("jealousy's a proof of love"), IV.136 ("love may be expelled by other love"), and IV.142 ("constancy deserves reward").

SERAPION.   These Romans will o'erhear us.
But who's that stranger? By his warlike port,
His fierce demeanor, and erected look,   90
He's of no vulgar note.
ALEXAS.   Oh, 'tis Ventidius,
Our emp'ror's great lieutenant in the East,
Who first showed Rome that Parthia could be conquered.
When Antony returned from Syria last,
He left this man to guard the Roman frontiers.   95
SERAPION.
You seem to know him well.
ALEXAS.
Too well. I saw him in Cilicia first,
When Cleopatra there met Antony:
A mortal foe he was to us, and Egypt.
But, let me witness to the worth I hate,   100
A braver Roman never drew a sword;
Firm to his prince, but as a friend, not slave.
He ne'er was of his pleasures, but presides
O'er all his cooler hours and morning counsels.
In short, the plainness, fierceness, rugged virtue   105
Of an old true-stamped Roman lives in him.
His coming bodes I know not what of ill
To our affairs. Withdraw, to mark him better;
And I'll acquaint you why I sought you here,
And what's our present work.

They withdraw to a corner of the stage; and Ventidius, *with the
other, comes forwards to the front.*

VENTIDIUS.   Not see him, say you?   110
I say I must, and will.
GENTLEMAN.   He has commanded,
On pain of death, none should approach his presence.

---

93. *Parthia*] In 53 B.C. the Roman general Marcus Crassus was killed
at Carrhae in a disastrous campaign against the Parthians. Ventidius
won brilliant victories against them in 39 and 38 B.C.
97. *Cilicia*] In 41 B.C. Antony summoned Cleopatra to Tarsus, in Cilicia,
to account for her actions in the war against Brutus and Cassius. Her
response was her famous appearance on her barge (III.162–182).

VENTIDIUS.

 I bring him news will raise his drooping spirits,
 Give him new life.

GENTLEMAN.   He sees not Cleopatra.

VENTIDIUS.

 Would he had never seen her!   115

GENTLEMAN.

 He eats not, drinks not, sleeps not, has no use
 Of anything but thought; or, if he talks,
 'Tis to himself, and then 'tis perfect raving.
 Then he defies the world, and bids it pass;
 Sometimes he gnaws his lip, and curses loud   120
 The boy Octavius; then he draws his mouth
 Into a scornful smile, and cries, "Take all,
 The world's not worth my care."

VENTIDIUS.   Just, just his nature.

 Virtue's his path; but sometimes 'tis too narrow
 For his vast soul, and then he starts out wide   125
 And bounds into a vice that bears him far
 From his first course, and plunges him in ills.
 But when his danger makes him find his fault,
 Quick to observe, and full of sharp remorse,
 He censures eagerly his own misdeeds,   130
 Judging himself with malice to himself,
 And not forgiving what as man he did
 Because his other parts are more than man.
 He must not thus be lost.

    Alexas *and the* Priests *come forward.*

ALEXAS.

 You have your full instructions, now advance;   135
 Proclaim your orders loudly.

SERAPION.

 Romans, Egyptians, hear the queen's command!

134.1. Priests] *Q1–2;* Priest *Q3,*
C1.

---

121. *The boy Octavius*] at this time thirty-three years old, twenty
years younger than Antony.

Thus Cleopatra bids: "Let labor cease.
To pomp and triumphs give this happy day
That gave the world a lord: 'tis Antony's."   140
Live, Antony; and Cleopatra live!
Be this the general voice sent up to heav'n,
And every public place repeat this echo.

VENTIDIUS *(aside).*

    Fine pageantry!

SERAPION.   Set out before your doors
The images of all your sleeping fathers,   145
With laurels crowned; with laurels wreathe your posts,
And strow with flow'rs the pavement; let the priests
Do present sacrifice; pour out the wine,
And call the gods to join with you in gladness.

VENTIDIUS.

Curse on the tongue that bids this general joy!   150
Can they be friends of Antony, who revel
When Antony's in danger? Hide, for shame,
You Romans, your great grandsires' images,
For fear their souls should animate their marbles
To blush at their degenerate progeny.   155

ALEXAS.

A love which knows no bounds to Antony
Would mark the day with honors, when all heaven
Labored for him, when each propitious star
Stood wakeful in his orb to watch that hour
And shed his better influence. Her own birthday   160
Our queen neglected, like a vulgar fate
That passed obscurely by.

VENTIDIUS.   Would it had slept,
Divided far from his, till some remote
And future age had called it out, to ruin
Some other prince, not him!

---

145. *images . . . fathers*] the *imagines,* or portrait masks of distinguished ancestors, which were kept in the homes of noble Roman
families.
148. *present*] immediate.
160. *influence*] in the astrological sense.

ALEXAS.   Your emperor,   165
     Though grown unkind, would be more gentle than
     T'upbraid my queen for loving him too well.
VENTIDIUS.
     Does the mute sacrifice upbraid the priest?
     He knows him not his executioner.
     Oh, she has decked his ruin with her love,   170
     Led him in golden bands to gaudy slaughter,
     And made perdition pleasing. She has left him
     The blank of what he was.
     I tell thee, eunuch, she has quite unmanned him.
     Can any Roman see and know him now,   175
     Thus altered from the lord of half mankind,
     Unbent, unsinewed, made a woman's toy,
     Shrunk from the vast extent of all his honors,
     And cramped within a corner of the world?
     O Antony!   180
     Thou bravest soldier, and thou best of friends!
     Bounteous as nature; next to nature's God!
     Couldst thou but make new worlds, so wouldst thou give 'em
     As bounty were thy being. Rough in battle
     As the first Romans when they went to war;   185
     Yet, after victory, more pitiful
     Than all their praying virgins left at home!
ALEXAS.
     Would you could add, to those more shining virtues,
     His truth to her who loves him.
VENTIDIUS.   Would I could not!
     But wherefore waste I precious hours with thee?   190
     Thou art her darling mischief, her chief engine,
     Antony's other fate. Go, tell thy queen
     Ventidius is arrived to end her charms.
     Let your Egyptian timbrels play alone,
     Nor mix effeminate sounds with Roman trumpets.   195
     You dare not fight for Antony; go pray,
     And keep your coward's holiday in temples.
                          Exeunt Alexas, Serapion.

174. quite] *Q1; om. Q2–3, C1.*

[*Enter a* Second] Gentleman *of Mark Antony.*

SECOND GENTLEMAN.

The emperor approaches, and commands,
On pain of death, that none presume to stay.

FIRST GENTLEMAN.

I dare not disobey him.   *Going out with the other.*
VENTIDIUS.   Well, I dare.   200
But I'll observe him first unseen, and find
Which way his humor drives. The rest I'll venture.

                                        Withdraws.

Enter Antony, *walking with a disturbed motion before he speaks.*

ANTONY.

They tell me 'tis my birthday, and I'll keep it
With double pomp of sadness.
'Tis what the day deserves which gave me breath.   205
Why was I raised the meteor of the world,
Hung in the skies, and blazing as I traveled,
Till all my fires were spent, and then cast downward
To be trod out by Caesar?
VENTIDIUS *(aside).*   On my soul,
'Tis mournful, wondrous mournful!

ANTONY.   Count thy gains.   210
Now, Antony, wouldst thou be born for this?
Glutton of fortune, thy devouring youth
Has starved thy wanting age.
VENTIDIUS *(aside).*   How sorrow shakes him!
So, now the tempest tears him up by th' roots,
And on the ground extends the noble ruin.   215
ANTONY *(having thrown himself down).*
Lie there, thou shadow of an emperor.
The place thou pressest on thy mother earth

197.2. *Enter a* Second] *Noyes; Re-*
enter the Q1–3, C1. (The First
Gentleman has not left the stage.)
197.2. Gentleman] *Q1–2;* Gentlemen *Q3, C1.*
202. The rest] *Q1–2; om. Q3, C1.*

216–227. Lie . . . on't] *Mistaking*
l. 216 S.P. and S.D. for a stage di-
rection alone, Q3 and C1 print
these lines as a continuation of
Ventidius's preceding speech. C1
inserts a speech prefix assigning
ll. 228 ff to Antony.

Is all thy empire now. Now it contains thee:
Some few days hence, and then 'twill be too large,
When thou'rt contracted in thy narrow urn,   220
Shrunk to a few cold ashes. Then Octavia
(For Cleopatra will not live to see it),
Octavia then will have thee all her own,
And bear thee in her widowed hand to Caesar.
Caesar will weep, the crocodile will weep,   225
To see his rival of the universe
Lie still and peaceful there. I'll think no more on't.
Give me some music; look that it be sad.
I'll soothe my melancholy till I swell
And burst myself with sighing.—   *Soft music.* 230
'Tis somewhat to my humor. Stay, I fancy
I'm now turned wild, a commoner of nature;
Of all forsaken, and forsaking all,
Live in a shady forest's sylvan scene,
Stretched at my length beneath some blasted oak.   235
I lean my head upon the mossy bark,
And look just of a piece, as I grew from it;
My uncombed locks, matted like mistletoe,
Hang o'er my hoary face; a murm'ring brook
Runs at my foot.
VENTIDIUS.   Methinks I fancy   240
Myself there too.
ANTONY.   The herd come jumping by me,

220. thy] *Q1-2*; the *Q3, C1.*

228-231. *Give . . . humor*] recalls the well-known opening speech of
the sentimental Duke Orsino in *Twelfth Night,* I.i.1-7 ("If music be
the food of love, play on," etc.). But see also *Antony and Cleopatra,*
II.v.1-2.
231-244. *Stay . . . thoughts*] echoes the description of "the melancholy
Jaques" in *As You Like It,* II.i.25-63.
234. *sylvan scene*] a phrase used to describe the Garden of Eden in
Milton's *Paradise Lost* (IV.140) and Dryden's *The State of Innocence*
(II.i.138).
241-243. *herd . . . fellow-citizen*] with possibly a hint of cuckoldry,
since the "herd" would have horns, and traditionally the attractive
wives of wealthy London merchants ("citizens") were seduced by
Charles II's courtiers.

And, fearless, quench their thirst while I look on,
And take me for their fellow-citizen.
More of this image, more; it lulls my thoughts.

Soft music again.

VENTIDIUS.

I must disturb him; I can hold no longer.   245

Stands before him.

ANTONY *(starting up).*

Art thou Ventidius?

VENTIDIUS.   Are you Antony?
I'm liker what I was, than you to him
I left you last.

ANTONY.   I'm angry.

VENTIDIUS.   So am I.

ANTONY.

I would be private. Leave me.

VENTIDIUS.   Sir, I love you,
And therefore will not leave you.

ANTONY.   Will not leave me?   250
Where have you learnt that answer? Who am I?

VENTIDIUS.

My emperor; the man I love next heaven;
If I said more, I think 'twere scarce a sin—
Y'are all that's good, and good-like.

ANTONY.   All that's wretched.
You will not leave me then?

VENTIDIUS.   'Twas too presuming   255
To say I would not; but I dare not leave you,
And 'tis unkind in you to chide me hence
So soon, when I so far have come to see you.

ANTONY.

Now thou hast seen me, art thou satisfied?
For, if a friend, thou hast beheld enough;   260
And, if a foe, too much.

VENTIDIUS *(weeping).*

Look, emperor, this is no common dew.

244. it] *Q1-2; om. Q3, C1.*   259. me] *Q1-2; om. Q3,C1.*
254. good-like] *Q1-4, C1;* god-like   260. hast beheld] *Q1-2;* hast seen
Q5, C2.   me, beheld *Q3,C1.*

I have not wept this forty year, but now
My mother comes afresh into my eyes;
I cannot help her softness.   265

ANTONY.

By heav'n, he weeps, poor good old man, he weeps!
The big round drops course one another down
The furrows of his cheeks. —Stop 'em, Ventidius,
Or I shall blush to death: they set my shame,
That caused 'em, full before me.

VENTIDIUS.   I'll do my best.   270

ANTONY.

Sure there's contagion in the tears of friends:
See, I have caught it too. Believe me, 'tis not
For my own griefs, but thine. —Nay, father!

VENTIDIUS.   Emperor!

ANTONY.

Emperor? Why, that's the style of victory.
The conqu'ring soldier, red with unfelt wounds,   275
Salutes his general so; but never more
Shall that sound reach my ears.

VENTIDIUS.   I warrant you.

ANTONY.

Actium, Actium! Oh!—

VENTIDIUS.   It sits too near you.

ANTONY.

Here, here it lies, a lump of lead by day,
And in my short, distracted nightly slumbers,   280
The hag that rides my dreams.—

VENTIDIUS.

Out with it; give it vent.

ANTONY.   Urge not my shame:
I lost a battle.

VENTIDIUS.   So has Julius done.

263. year] *Q1; years Q2–3, C1.*

---

281. *hag*] in popular superstition, a female spirit ("nightmare") believed to cause bad dreams by riding the victim.

ANTONY.

Thou favor'st me, and speak'st not half thou think'st;
For Julius fought it out, and lost it fairly,   285
But Antony—
VENTIDIUS.   Nay, stop not.
ANTONY.   Antony—
Well, thou wilt have it—like a coward, fled,
Fled while his soldiers fought; fled first, Ventidius.
Thou long'st to curse me, and I give thee leave.
I know thou cam'st prepared to rail.
VENTIDIUS.   I did.   290
ANTONY.

I'll help thee. —I have been a man, Ventidius—
VENTIDIUS.

Yes, and a brave one; but—
ANTONY.   I know thy meaning.
But I have lost my reason, have disgraced
The name of soldier with inglorious ease.
In the full vintage of my flowing honors,   295
Sat still, and saw it pressed by other hands.
Fortune came smiling to my youth, and wooed it,
And purple greatness met my ripened years.
When first I came to empire, I was borne
On tides of people, crowding to my triumphs,   300
The wish of nations! and the willing world
Received me as its pledge of future peace.
I was so great, so happy, so beloved,
Fate could not ruin me; till I took pains
And worked against my fortune, chid her from me,   305
And turned her loose; yet still she came again.
My careless days and my luxurious nights
At length have wearied her, and now she's gone,
Gone, gone, divorced forever. Help me, soldier,
To curse this madman, this industrious fool,   310
Who labored to be wretched: prithee, curse me.

285. fought] *Q1–2,C1;* sought *Q3.*   290. cam'st] *Q1; com'st Q2–3,C1.*
289. thee] *Q1,Q3,C1;* the *Q2.*   298. purple] *Q1–3;* purpled *C1.*

VENTIDIUS.

No.

ANTONY. Why?

VENTIDIUS.   You are too sensible already
Of what y'have done, too conscious of your failings,
And like a scorpion, whipped by others first
To fury, sting yourself in mad revenge.   315
I would bring balm, and pour it in your wounds;
Cure your distempered mind, and heal your fortunes.

ANTONY.

I know thou wouldst.

VENTIDIUS.   I will.

ANTONY.   Ha, ha, ha, ha!

VENTIDIUS.

You laugh.

ANTONY.   I do, to see officious love
Give cordials to the dead.

VENTIDIUS.   You would be lost, then?   320

ANTONY.

I am.

VENTIDIUS.   I say you are not. Try your fortune.

ANTONY.

I have, to th'utmost. Dost thou think me desperate
Without just cause? No, when I found all lost
Beyond repair, I hid me from the world,
And learnt to scorn it here; which now I do   325
So heartily, I think it is not worth
The cost of keeping.

VENTIDIUS.   Caesar thinks not so:
He'll thank you for the gift he could not take.
You would be killed like Tully, would you? Do,
Hold out your throat to Caesar, and die tamely.   330

ANTONY.

No, I can kill myself; and so resolve.

---

329. *Tully*] When Cicero, condemned to death by the triumvirate in
43 B.C., was overtaken by the soldiers of Antony, he forbade his ser-
vants to resist and offered his neck to his executioners.

VENTIDIUS.

I can die with you, too, when time shall serve,
But fortune calls upon us now to live,
To fight, to conquer.
ANTONY.   Sure thou dream'st, Ventidius.
VENTIDIUS.

No, 'tis you dream; you sleep away your hours   335
In desperate sloth, miscalled philosophy.
Up, up, for honor's sake! Twelve legions wait you,
And long to call you chief. By painful journeys
I led 'em, patient both of heat and hunger,
Down from the Parthian marches to the Nile.   340
'Twill do you good to see their sunburnt faces,
Their scarred cheeks, and chopped hands. There's virtue
                                              in 'em:
They'll sell those mangled limbs at dearer rates
Than yon trim bands can buy.
ANTONY.   Where left you them?
VENTIDIUS.

I said in Lower Syria.
ANTONY.   Bring 'em hither;   345
There may be life in these.
VENTIDIUS.   They will not come.
ANTONY.

Why didst thou mock my hopes with promised aids
To double my despair? They're mutinous.
VENTIDIUS.

Most firm and loyal.
ANTONY.   Yet they will not march
To succor me. O trifler!
VENTIDIUS.   They petition   350
You would make haste to head 'em.
ANTONY.   I'm besieged.

335. hours] *Q1–3*; hour *C1*.

---

340. *marches*] frontiers.
342. *chopped*] chapped.
344. *yon trim bands*] Octavius's forces.

VENTIDIUS.
   There's but one way shut up: how came I hither?
ANTONY.
   I will not stir.
VENTIDIUS.   They would perhaps desire
   A better reason.
ANTONY.   I have never used
   My soldiers to demand a reason of   355
   My actions. Why did they refuse to march?
VENTIDIUS.
   They said they would not fight for Cleopatra.
ANTONY.
   What was't they said?
VENTIDIUS.
   They said they would not fight for Cleopatra.
   Why should they fight, indeed, to make her conquer,   360
   And make you more a slave? to gain you kingdoms,
   Which, for a kiss at your next midnight feast,
   You'll sell to her? Then she new-names her jewels,
   And calls this diamond such or such a tax;
   Each pendant in her ear shall be a province.   365
ANTONY.
   Ventidius, I allow your tongue free license
   On all my other faults; but, on your life,
   No word of Cleopatra. She deserves
   More worlds than I can lose.
VENTIDIUS.   Behold, you pow'rs,
   To whom you have intrusted humankind;   370
   See Europe, Afric, Asia put in balance,
   And all weighed down by one light, worthless woman!
   I think the gods are Antonies, and give,
   Like prodigals, this nether world away
   To none but wasteful hands.
ANTONY.   You grow presumptuous.   375

372. worthless] *Q1–2,C1;* wrothless
Q3.

_____

354. *used*] accustomed.

VENTIDIUS.

    I take the privilege of plain love to speak.

ANTONY.

    Plain love? Plain arrogance, plain insolence!
    Thy men are cowards, thou an envious traitor
    Who, under seeming honesty, hast vented
    The burden of thy rank, o'erflowing gall.   380
    Oh, that thou wert my equal, great in arms
    As the first Caesar was, that I might kill thee
    Without a stain to honor!

VENTIDIUS.   You may kill me.

    You have done more already: called me traitor.

ANTONY.

    Art thou not one?

VENTIDIUS.   For showing you yourself,   385
    Which none else durst have done? But had I been
    That name, which I disdain to speak again,
    I needed not have sought your abject fortunes,
    Come to partake your fate, to die with you.
    What hindered me t'have led my conqu'ring eagles   390
    To fill Octavius' bands? I could have been
    A traitor then, a glorious, happy traitor,
    And not have been so called.

ANTONY.   Forgive me, soldier:
    I've been too passionate.

VENTIDIUS.   You thought me false;
    Thought my old age betrayed you. Kill me, sir;   395
    Pray, kill me. Yet you need not; your unkindness
    Has left your sword no work.

ANTONY.   I did not think so;
    I said it in my rage; prithee forgive me.
    Why didst thou tempt my anger by discovery
    Of what I would not hear?

VENTIDIUS.   No prince but you   400
    Could merit that sincerity I used,
    Nor durst another man have ventured it.

---

378. Thy] *Q1–2;* The *Q3,C1.*   389. you.] *Q2–3,C1;* you, *Q1.*

But you, ere love misled your wand'ring eyes,
Were sure the chief and best of human race,
Framed in the very pride and boast of nature,   405
So perfect, that the gods who formed you wondered
At their own skill, and cried, "A lucky hit
Has mended our design." Their envy hindered,
Else you had been immortal, and a pattern,
When heav'n would work for ostentation sake,   410
To copy out again.

ANTONY.   But Cleopatra—
Go on, for I can bear it now.

VENTIDIUS.   No more.

ANTONY.
Thou dar'st not trust my passion, but thou mayst;
Thou only lov'st, the rest have flattered me.

VENTIDIUS.
Heav'n's blessing on your heart for that kind word!   415
May I believe you love me? Speak again.

ANTONY.
Indeed I do. Speak this, and this, and this. *Hugging him.*
Thy praises were unjust, but I'll deserve 'em,
And yet mend all. Do with me what thou wilt;
Lead me to victory! Thou know'st the way.   420

VENTIDIUS.
And—will you leave this—

ANTONY.   Prithee, do not curse her,
And I will leave her; though, heav'n knows, I love
Beyond life, conquest, empire, all but honor;
But I will leave her.

VENTIDIUS.   That's my royal master.
And—shall we fight?

ANTONY.   I warrant thee, old soldier,   425
Thou shalt behold me once again in iron,
And at the head of our old troops that beat
The Parthians, cry aloud, "Come, follow me!"

VENTIDIUS.
Oh, now I hear my emp'ror! In that word

403. you] *Q1-2,C1;* your *Q3.*

Octavius fell. Gods, let me see that day,   430
And if I have ten years behind, take all;
I'll thank you for th'exchange.
ANTONY.   O Cleopatra!
VENTIDIUS.
   Again?
ANTONY.   I've done. In that last sigh, she went.
   Caesar shall know what 'tis to force a lover
   From all he holds most dear.
VENTIDIUS.   Methinks you breathe   435
   Another soul: your looks are more divine;
   You speak a hero, and you move a god.
ANTONY.
   Oh, thou hast fired me; my soul's up in arms,
   And mans each part about me. Once again
   That noble eagerness of fight has seized me,   440
   That eagerness with which I darted upward
   To Cassius' camp. In vain the steepy hill
   Opposed my way; in vain a war of spears
   Sung round my head, and planted all my shield.
   I won the trenches while my foremost men   445
   Lagged on the plain below.
VENTIDIUS.   Ye gods, ye gods,
   For such another hour!
ANTONY.   Come on, my soldier!
   Our hearts and arms are still the same. I long
   Once more to meet our foes, that thou and I,
   Like Time and Death, marching before our troops,   450
   May taste fate to 'em; mow 'em out a passage,
       And ent'ring where the foremost squadrons yield,
       Begin the noble harvest of the field.   *Exeunt.*

447. hour] *Q1-2;* honor *Q3,C1.*

---

442. *Cassius' camp*] in 42 B.C. at Philippi, where Antony and Octavius
defeated Brutus and Cassius.
451. *taste*] like an official "taster" of food and drink for a monarch.

ACT II

Cleopatra, Iras, *and* Alexas.

CLEOPATRA.

What shall I do, or whither shall I turn?
Ventidius has o'ercome, and he will go.

ALEXAS.

He goes to fight for you.

CLEOPATRA.

Then he would see me ere he went to fight.
Flatter me not: if once he goes, he's lost,   5
And all my hopes destroyed.

ALEXAS.   Does this weak passion
Become a mighty queen?

CLEOPATRA.   I am no queen.
Is this to be a queen, to be besieged
By yon insulting Roman, and to wait
Each hour the victor's chain? These ills are small;   10
For Antony is lost, and I can mourn
For nothing else but him. Now come, Octavius,
I have no more to lose; prepare thy bands;
I'm fit to be a captive: Antony
Has taught my mind the fortune of a slave.   15

IRAS.

Call reason to assist you.

CLEOPATRA.   I have none,
And none would have. My love's a noble madness,
Which shows the cause deserved it. Moderate sorrow
Fits vulgar love, and for a vulgar man;
But I have loved with such transcendent passion,   20
I soared at first quite out of reason's view,
And now am lost above it. No, I'm proud
'Tis thus. Would Antony could see me now!
Think you he would not sigh? Though he must leave me,

0.1. Cleopatra] *Q1–2; Enter* Cleo-   7. no queen] *Q2–3,C1;* no qneen
patra *Q3,C1.*   *Q1.*

13. *bands*] bonds, fetters.

Sure he would sigh, for he is noble-natured,   25
And bears a tender heart: I know him well.
Ah, no, I know him not; I knew him once,
But now 'tis past.
IRAS.   Let it be past with you:
Forget him, madam.
CLEOPATRA.   Never, never, Iras.
He once was mine; and once, though now 'tis gone,   30
Leaves a faint image of possession still.
ALEXAS.
Think him unconstant, cruel, and ungrateful.
CLEOPATRA.
I cannot. If I could, those thoughts were vain.
Faithless, ungrateful, cruel though he be,
I still must love him.

Enter Charmion.

                    Now, what news, my Charmion?   35
Will he be kind? and will he not forsake me?
Am I to live, or die?—nay, do I live,
Or am I dead? for when he gave his answer,
Fate took the word, and then I lived or died.
CHARMION.
I found him, madam—
CLEOPATRA.   A long speech preparing?   40
If thou bring'st comfort, haste, and give it me,
For never was more need.
IRAS.   I know he loves you.
CLEOPATRA.
Had he been kind, her eyes had told me so
Before her tongue could speak it. Now she studies
To soften what he said; but give me death   45
Just as he sent it, Charmion, undisguised,
And in the words he spoke.
CHARMION.   I found him, then,
Incompassed round, I think, with iron statues,
So mute, so motionless his soldiers stood
While awfully he cast his eyes about,   50

And every leader's hopes or fears surveyed.
Methought he looked resolved, and yet not pleased.
When he beheld me struggling in the crowd,
He blushed, and bade make way.

ALEXAS.   There's comfort yet.

CHARMION.

Ventidius fixed his eyes upon my passage   55
Severely, as he meant to frown me back,
And sullenly gave place. I told my message
Just as you gave it, broken and disordered.
I numbered in it all your sighs and tears,
And while I moved your pitiful request   60
That you but only begged a last farewell,
He fetched an inward groan, and every time
I named you, sighed as if his heart were breaking,
But shunned my eyes, and guiltily looked down.
He seemed not now that awful Antony   65
Who shook an armed assembly with his nod,
But making show as he would rub his eyes,
Disguised and blotted out a falling tear.

CLEOPATRA.

Did he then weep? and was I worth a tear?
If what thou hast to say be not as pleasing,   70
Tell me no more, but let me die contented.

CHARMION.

He bid me say, he knew himself so well,
He could deny you nothing if he saw you,
And therefore—

CLEOPATRA.   Thou wouldst say, he would not see me?

CHARMION.

And therefore begged you not to use a power   75
Which he could ill resist; yet he should ever
Respect you as he ought.

CLEOPATRA.   Is that a word
For Antony to use to Cleopatra?
O that faint word, "respect"! How I disdain it!

---

62. fetched] *Q1,Q3,C1;* fetch *Q2.*   74. wouldst] *Q1,Q3,C1;* would *Q2.*
65. that] *Q1–2;* the *Q3,C1.*

Disdain myself, for loving after it!   80
He should have kept that word for cold Octavia.
Respect is for a wife: am I that thing,
That dull, insipid lump, without desires,
And without pow'r to give 'em?
ALEXAS.   You misjudge.
You see through love, and that deludes your sight,   85
As what is straight seems crooked through the water.
But I, who bear my reason undisturbed,
Can see this Antony, this dreaded man,
A fearful slave who fain would run away,
And shuns his master's eyes. If you pursue him,   90
My life on't, he still drags a chain along
That needs must clog his flight.
CLEOPATRA.   Could I believe thee!—
ALEXAS.
By every circumstance I know he loves.
True, he's hard pressed by int'rest and by honor;
Yet he but doubts, and parleys, and casts out   95
Many a long look for succor.
CLEOPATRA.   He sends word
He fears to see my face.
ALEXAS.   And would you more?
He shows his weakness who declines the combat,
And you must urge your fortune. Could he speak
More plainly? To my ears the message sounds: 100
"Come to my rescue, Cleopatra, come;
Come, free me from Ventidius, from my tyrant;
See me, and give me a pretense to leave him!"
I hear his trumpets. This way he must pass.
Please you, retire a while; I'll work him first,   105
That he may bend more easy.
CLEOPATRA.   You shall rule me;
But all, I fear, in vain.
                    Exit with Charmion *and* Iras.
ALEXAS.   I fear so too,

95. casts] *Q1–3;* cast *C1.*   96. look] *Q1;* lookt *Q2;* look't *Q3;*
                                        look'd *C1.*

Though I concealed my thoughts to make her bold.
But 'tis our utmost means, and fate befriend it! *Withdraws.*

Enter lictors with fasces, one bearing the eagle; then enter Antony
with Ventidius, *followed by other commanders.*

ANTONY.
Octavius is the minion of blind chance,   110
But holds from virtue nothing.
VENTIDIUS.   Has he courage?
ANTONY.
But just enough to season him from coward.
Oh, 'tis the coldest youth upon a charge,
The most deliberate fighter! If he ventures
(As in Illyria once they say he did,   115
To storm a town), 'tis when he cannot choose,
When all the world have fixed their eyes upon him;
And then he lives on that for seven years after.
But at a close revenge he never fails.
VENTIDIUS.
I heard you challenged him.
ANTONY.   I did, Ventidius.   120
What think'st thou was his answer? 'Twas so tame!
He said he had more ways than one to die;
I had not.
VENTIDIUS.   Poor!
ANTONY.   He has more ways than one,
But he would choose 'em all before that one.

122. one] *Q1–2; om. Q3,C1.*

---

111. *Has he courage?*] "The following lines have been held to be a
slur upon Louis XIV for physical cowardice. The king of France
began his wars for European supremacy in 1672 and thus gave the
dramatists of England a reason for satiric allusion" (David Harrison
Stevens, ed., *Types of English Drama, 1660–1780,* Boston, 1923, p. 884).
115–116. *As . . . town*] at the siege of Metulus during Octavius's
Illyrian campaigns in 35–34 B.C.
119. *close*] secret.
122. *more . . . die*] Dryden follows Shakespeare's misunderstanding
(Antony and Cleopatra, IV.i.5) of an ambiguous passage in North's
Plutarch: "Caesar answered him that he [i.e., Antony] had many
other ways to die than so."

VENTIDIUS.

He first would choose an ague or a fever.   125
ANTONY.

No, it must be an ague, not a fever:
He has not warmth enough to die by that.
VENTIDIUS.

Or old age and a bed.
ANTONY.   Ay, there's his choice.
He would live, like a lamp, to the last wink,
And crawl upon the utmost verge of life.   130
O Hercules! Why should a man like this,
Who dares not trust his fate for one great action,
Be all the care of heav'n? Why should he lord it
O'er fourscore thousand men, of whom each one
Is braver than himself?
VENTIDIUS.   You conquered for him.   135
Philippi knows it; there you shared with him
That empire which your sword made all your own.
ANTONY.

Fool that I was, upon my eagle's wings
I bore this wren till I was tired with soaring,
And now he mounts above me.   140
Good heav'ns, is this—is this the man who braves me?
Who bids my age make way, drives me before him
To the world's ridge, and sweeps me off like rubbish?
VENTIDIUS.

Sir, we lose time; the troops are mounted all.
ANTONY.

Then give the word to march.   145
I long to leave this prison of a town,

---

131. *Hercules*] Antony traced his descent to Hercules, whom he was
thought to resemble in appearance, and whom he imitated in bearing
and attire. See also II.206, II.393, III.13–16, III.41–42.
136. *Philippi*] where, nearly defeated by the army of Brutus, Octavius's
forces were rescued by Antony, who had already defeated Cassius.
139. *bore this wren*] alluding to the fable of the wren who surpassed
the eagle in a contest by first flying upward concealed in the eagle's
feathers.

To join thy legions, and in open field
Once more to show my face. Lead, my deliverer.

Enter Alexas.

ALEXAS.

Great emperor,
In mighty arms renowned above mankind,   150
But, in soft pity to th'oppressed, a god,
This message sends the mournful Cleopatra
To her departing lord.

VENTIDIUS.   Smooth sycophant!

ALEXAS.

A thousand wishes and ten thousand prayers,
Millions of blessings wait you to the wars.   155
Millions of sighs and tears she sends you too,
And would have sent
As many dear embraces to your arms,
As many parting kisses to your lips,
But those, she fears, have wearied you already.   160

VENTIDIUS *(aside)*.

False crocodile!

ALEXAS.

And yet she begs not now you would not leave her.
That were a wish too mighty for her hopes,
Too presuming
For her low fortune, and your ebbing love;   165
That were a wish for her more prosp'rous days,
Her blooming beauty, and your growing kindness.

ANTONY *(aside)*.

Well, I must man it out.—What would the queen?

ALEXAS.

First, to these noble warriors, who attend
Your daring courage in the chase of fame—   170
Too daring and too dang'rous for her quiet—
She humbly recommends all she holds dear,
All her own cares and fears: the care of you.

164–165. Too . . . love] *printed as
one line in Q1–3,C1.*

VENTIDIUS.

   Yes, witness Actium.

ANTONY.   Let him speak, Ventidius.

ALEXAS.

   You, when his matchless valor bears him forward,   175
With ardor too heroic, on his foes,
Fall down, as she would do, before his feet;
Lie in his way, and stop the paths of death.
Tell him this god is not invulnerable,
That absent Cleopatra bleeds in him;   180
And, that you may remember her petition,
She begs you wear these trifles as a pawn
Which, at your wished return, she will redeem

                 Gives jewels to the commanders.

With all the wealth of Egypt.
This to the great Ventidius she presents,   185
Whom she can never count her enemy,
Because he loves her lord.

VENTIDIUS.   Tell her I'll none on't.

   I'm not ashamed of honest poverty.
Not all the diamonds of the East can bribe
Ventidius from his faith. I hope to see   190
These, and the rest of all her sparkling store,
Where they shall more deservingly be placed.

ANTONY.

   And who must wear 'em then?

VENTIDIUS.   The wronged Octavia.

ANTONY.

   You might have spared that word.

VENTIDIUS.   And he that bribe.

ANTONY.

   But have I no remembrance?

ALEXAS.   Yes, a dear one: 195

   Your slave, the queen—

ANTONY.   My mistress.

ALEXAS.   Then your mistress;

   Your mistress would, she says, have sent her soul,
But that you had long since. She humbly begs
This ruby bracelet, set with bleeding hearts,

The emblems of her own, may bind your arm.   200

Presenting a bracelet.

VENTIDIUS.

Now, my best lord, in honor's name I ask you,
For manhood's sake, and for your own dear safety,
Touch not these poisoned gifts,
Infected by the sender; touch 'em not.
Myriads of bluest plagues lie underneath 'em,   205
And more than aconite has dipped the silk.

ANTONY.

Nay, now you grow too cynical, Ventidius:
A lady's favors may be worn with honor.
What, to refuse her bracelet! On my soul,
When I lie pensive in my tent alone,   210
'Twill pass the wakeful hours of winter nights
To tell these pretty beads upon my arm,
To count for every one a soft embrace,
A melting kiss at such and such a time,
And now and then the fury of her love   215
When— And what harm's in this?

ALEXAS.   None, none, my lord,
But what's to her, that now 'tis past forever.

ANTONY *(going to tie it)*.
We soldiers are so awkward. —Help me tie it.

ALEXAS.

In faith, my lord, we courtiers too are awkward
In these affairs. So are all men indeed;   220
Ev'n I, who am not one. But shall I speak?

ANTONY.

Yes, freely.

215. love] love. *Q1–3,C1.*

---

206. *aconite . . . silk*] possibly alluding to the death of Hercules,
Antony's supposed ancestor, who was poisoned and driven mad by
putting on the bloody shirt of Nessus, a centaur he had killed.
Deianira had given him the shirt in hopes of gaining his love.
208. *favors*] in medieval chivalry, worn by a knight as a token of his
lady's affection, as for example a glove or a knot of ribbons.

ALEXAS.   Then, my lord, fair hands alone
Are fit to tie it; she who sent it can.

VENTIDIUS.

Hell, death! this eunuch pander ruins you.
You will not see her?

             Alexas whispers an attendant, who goes out.

ANTONY.   But to take my leave.   225

VENTIDIUS.

Then I have washed an Aethiope. Y'are undone;
Y'are in the toils; y'are taken; y'are destroyed.
Her eyes do Caesar's work.

ANTONY.   You fear too soon.
I'm constant to myself, I know my strength,
And yet she shall not think me barbarous neither,   230
Born in the depths of Afric. I'm a Roman,
Bred to the rules of soft humanity.
A guest, and kindly used, should bid farewell.

VENTIDIUS.

You do not know
How weak you are to her, how much an infant.   235
You are not proof against a smile or glance:
A sigh will quite disarm you.

ANTONY.   See, she comes!
Now you shall find your error. Gods, I thank you:
I formed the danger greater than it was,
And now 'tis near, 'tis lessened.

VENTIDIUS.   Mark the end yet.   240

        Enter Cleopatra, Charmion, *and* Iras.

ANTONY.

Well, madam, we are met.

CLEOPATRA.   Is this a meeting?
Then we must part?

230. neither,] *Q3,C1;* neither. *Q1–*   231. Roman,] *Q1,Q3,C1;* Roman.
2.   *Q2.*
                                      242. part?] *Q1–3;* part. *C1.*

---

226. *washed an Aethiope*] a proverbial expression for a hopeless endeavor.

ANTONY.   We must.

CLEOPATRA.   Who says we must?

ANTONY.
    Our own hard fates.

CLEOPATRA.   We make those fates ourselves.

ANTONY.
    Yes, we have made 'em; we have loved each other
    Into our mutual ruin.   245

CLEOPATRA.
    The gods have seen my joys with envious eyes;
    I have no friends in heav'n, and all the world,
    As 'twere the business of mankind to part us,
    Is armed against my love. Ev'n you yourself
    Join with the rest; you, you are armed against me.   250

ANTONY.
    I will be justified in all I do
    To late posterity, and therefore hear me.
    If I mix a lie
    With any truth, reproach me freely with it;
    Else favor me with silence.   You command me,   255
CLEOPATRA.
    And I am dumb.

VENTIDIUS.
    I like this well: he shows authority.

ANTONY.
    That I derive my ruin
    From you alone—

CLEOPATRA.   O heav'ns! I ruin you?

ANTONY.
    You promised me your silence, and you break it   260
    Ere I have scarce begun.

CLEOPATRA.   Well, I obey you.

ANTONY.
    When I beheld you first, it was in Egypt,

245. Into] *Q1–3*; In *C1*.

262–266. *When . . . ripen*] As commander of cavalry for Aulus Gabin-
ius, Antony helped restore Cleopatra's father, Ptolemy XII Auletes,
to the throne of Egypt in 55 B.C., when she was only fourteen years old.

Ere Caesar saw your eyes. You gave me love,
And were too young to know it. That I settled
Your father in his throne was for your sake; 265
I left th'acknowledgment for time to ripen.
Caesar stepped in, and with a greedy hand
Plucked the green fruit ere the first blush of red,
Yet cleaving to the bough. He was my lord,
And was, beside, too great for me to rival, 270
But I deserved you first, though he enjoyed you.
When, after, I beheld you in Cilicia
An enemy to Rome, I pardoned you.

CLEOPATRA.
    I cleared myself—

ANTONY.   Again you break your promise.
I loved you still, and took your weak excuses, 275
Took you into my bosom, stained by Caesar,
And not half mine. I went to Egypt with you,
And hid me from the business of the world,
Shut out enquiring nations from my sight,
To give whole years to you. 280

VENTIDIUS (aside).
    Yes, to your shame be't spoken.

ANTONY.   How I loved,
Witness ye days and nights, and all your hours
That danced away with down upon your feet,
As all your business were to count my passion!
One day passed by, and nothing saw but love; 285
Another came, and still 'twas only love.
The suns were wearied out with looking on,
And I untired with loving.
I saw you every day, and all the day,

263. eyes. You] eyes; you *Q1–2;*
eyes, you *Q3,C1.*

267–271. *Caesar . . . you*] Cleopatra became Julius Caesar's mistress
during his sojourn in Egypt over the winter of 48–47 B.C., while Antony
was in Rome. She resided in Rome for the eighteen months prior to
Caesar's assassination in 44 B.C.
272. *Cilicia*] See note to I.97, above.

And every day was still but as the first,   290
So eager was I still to see you more.

VENTIDIUS.
'Tis all too true.

ANTONY.   Fulvia, my wife, grew jealous,
As she indeed had reason; raised a war
In Italy, to call me back.

VENTIDIUS.   But yet
You went not.

ANTONY.   While within your arms I lay,   295
The world fell mold'ring from my hands each hour,
And left me scarce a grasp: I thank your love for't.

VENTIDIUS.
Well pushed: that last was home.

CLEOPATRA.   Yet may I speak?

ANTONY.
If I have urged a falsehood, yes; else, not.
Your silence says I have not. Fulvia died—   300
Pardon, you gods, with my unkindness died.
To set the world at peace I took Octavia,
This Caesar's sister; in her pride of youth
And flow'r of beauty did I wed that lady,
Whom blushing I must praise, because I left her.   305
You called; my love obeyed the fatal summons;
This raised the Roman arms; the cause was yours.
I would have fought by land, where I was stronger;
You hindered it, yet when I fought at sea,
Forsook me fighting, and—O stain to honor!   310
O lasting shame!—I knew not that I fled,
But fled to follow you.

VENTIDIUS.
What haste she made to hoist her purple sails!
And, to appear magnificent in flight,
Drew half our strength away.

300. Fulvia] *Q1,Q3,C1;* Fulvio *Q2.*

---

292. *Fulvia*] In 41 B.C. Fulvia, an ambitious, strong-minded woman, joined Antony's brother Lucius in making war against Octavius. She was defeated and died the following year.

ANTONY. All this you caused, 315
And would you multiply more ruins on me?
This honest man, my best, my only friend,
Has gathered up the shipwrack of my fortunes.
Twelve legions I have left, my last recruits,
And you have watched the news, and bring your eyes 320
To seize them too. If you have aught to answer,
Now speak, you have free leave.

ALEXAS (aside). She stands confounded.
Despair is in her eyes.

VENTIDIUS.
Now lay a sigh i'th' way to stop his passage;
Prepare a tear, and bid it for his legions: 325
'Tis like they shall be sold.

CLEOPATRA.
How shall I plead my cause when you, my judge,
Already have condemned me? Shall I bring
The love you bore me for my advocate?
That now is turned against me, that destroys me, 330
For love once past is at the best forgotten,
But oft'ner sours to hate. 'Twill please my lord
To ruin me, and therefore I'll be guilty.
But could I once have thought it would have pleased you,
That you would pry with narrow searching eyes 335
Into my faults, severe to my destruction,
And watching all advantages with care
That serve to make me wretched? Speak, my lord,
For I end here. Though I deserve this usage,
Was it like you to give it?

ANTONY. Oh, you wrong me 340
To think I sought this parting, or desired
T'accuse you more than what will clear myself
And justify this breach.

CLEOPATRA. Thus low I thank you,
And since my innocence will not offend,
I shall not blush to own it.

318. shipwrack] *Q1;* shipwreck   336. destruction,] destruction. *Q1;*
Q2–3,C1.   destruction: *Q2–3,C1.*
                                                          341. or] *Q1–3;* as *C1.*

VENTIDIUS. After this,   345
     I think she'll blush at nothing.

CLEOPATRA. You seem grieved
     (And therein you are kind) that Caesar first
     Enjoyed my love, though you deserved it better.
     I grieve for that, my lord, much more than you,
     For had I first been yours, it would have saved   350
     My second choice; I never had been his,
     And ne'er had been but yours. But Caesar first,
     You say, possessed my love. Not so, my lord:
     He first possessed my person, you my love;
     Caesar loved me, but I loved Antony.   355
     If I endured him after, 'twas because
     I judged it due to the first name of men,
     And half constrained, I gave, as to a tyrant,
     What he would take by force.

VENTIDIUS. O siren! siren!
     Yet grant that all the love she boasts were true,   360
     Has she not ruined you? I still urge that,
     The fatal consequence.

CLEOPATRA. The consequence indeed,
     For I dare challenge him, my greatest foe,
     To say it was designed. 'Tis true I loved you,
     And kept you far from an uneasy wife: 365
     Such Fulvia was.
     Yes, but he'll say you left Octavia for me;—
     And can you blame me to receive that love
     Which quitted such desert for worthless me?
     How often have I wished some other Caesar,   370
     Great as the first, and as the second young,
     Would court my love, to be refused for you!

VENTIDIUS.
     Words, words; but Actium, sir, remember Actium.

CLEOPATRA.
     Ev'n there I dare his malice. True, I counseled
     To fight at sea, but I betrayed you not.   375
     I fled, but not to th'enemy. 'Twas fear.

365. wife] *Q1–2;* will *Q3,C1.*

Would I had been a man, not to have feared!
For none would then have envied me your friendship,
Who envy me your love.
ANTONY.   We're both unhappy.
If nothing else, yet our ill fortune parts us.   380
Speak: would you have me perish by my stay?
CLEOPATRA.
If as a friend you ask my judgment, go;
If as a lover, stay. If you must perish—
'Tis a hard word—but stay.
VENTIDIUS.
See now th'effects of her so boasted love!   385
She strives to drag you down to ruin with her;
But could she 'scape without you, oh, how soon
Would she let go her hold, and haste to shore,
And never look behind!
CLEOPATRA.
Then judge my love by this.   *Giving* Antony a writing.
Could I have borne   390
A life or death, a happiness or woe
From yours divided, this had giv'n me means.
ANTONY.
By Hercules, the writing of Octavius!
I know it well; 'tis that proscribing hand,
Young as it was, that led the way to mine   395
And left me but the second place in murder.—
See, see, Ventidius! here he offers Egypt,
And joins all Syria to it as a present,
So, in requital, she forsake my fortunes
And join her arms with his.
CLEOPATRA.   And yet you leave me!   400
You leave me, Antony, and yet I love you,
Indeed I do. I have refused a kingdom;

394. proscribing] *Q1;* prescribing
Q2–3,C1

---

394. *proscribing*] In 43 B.C. Octavius, Antony, and Lepidus, who made
up the Second Triumvirate, condemned many of their enemies to
death. See the famous scene in Shakespeare's *Julius Caesar,* IV.i.

That's a trifle:
For I could part with life, with anything
But only you. Oh, let me die but with you!   405
Is that a hard request?

ANTONY.   Next living with you,
'Tis all that heav'n can give.

ALEXAS *(aside)*.   He melts; we conquer.

CLEOPATRA.

No; you shall go. Your int'rest calls you hence;
Yes, your dear int'rest pulls too strong for these
Weak arms to hold you here.—   *Takes his hand.*
Go, leave me, soldier   410
(For you're no more a lover), leave me dying;
Push me all pale and panting from your bosom,
And when your march begins, let one run after,
Breathless almost for joy, and cry, "She's dead."
The soldiers shout; you then perhaps may sigh,   415
And muster all your Roman gravity.
Ventidius chides, and straight your brow clears up,
As I had never been.

ANTONY.   Gods, 'tis too much,
Too much for man to bear!

CLEOPATRA.   What is't for me, then,
A weak, forsaken woman, and a lover?—   420
Here let me breathe my last. Envy me not
This minute in your arms: I'll die apace,
As fast as e'er I can, and end your trouble.

ANTONY.

Die? Rather let me perish! Loosened nature
Leap from its hinges, sink the props of heav'n,   425
And fall the skies to crush the nether world!
My eyes, my soul, my all!—   *Embraces her.*

VENTIDIUS.   And what's this toy
In balance with your fortune, honor, fame?

ANTONY.

What is't, Ventidius? It outweighs 'em all;
Why, we have more than conquered Caesar now.   430

418–419. Gods . . . bear] *printed*   419. bear] *Q1–2,C1;* beard *Q3.*
as one full line in Q1–3,C1.   429. is't] *Q1–2,C1;* it't *Q3.*

My queen's not only innocent, but loves me.
This, this is she who drags me down to ruin!
"But could she 'scape without me, with what haste
Would she let slip her hold, and make to shore,
And never look behind!"   435
Down on thy knees, blasphemer as thou art,
And ask forgiveness of wronged innocence.

VENTIDIUS.
 I'll rather die than take it. Will you go?

ANTONY.
 Go? Whither? Go from all that's excellent?
Faith, honor, virtue, all good things forbid   440
That I should go from her who sets my love
Above the price of kingdoms. Give, you gods,
Give to your boy, your Caesar,
This rattle of a globe to play withal,
This gewgaw world, and put him cheaply off;   445
I'll not be pleased with less than Cleopatra.

CLEOPATRA.
 She's wholly yours. My heart's so full of joy
That I shall do some wild extravagance
Of love in public, and the foolish world,
Which knows not tenderness, will think me mad.   450

VENTIDIUS.
 O women! women! women! all the gods
Have not such pow'r of doing good to man
As you of doing harm.   *Exit.*

ANTONY.   Our men are armed.
Unbar the gate that looks to Caesar's camp.
I would revenge the treachery he meant me,   455
And long security makes conquest easy.
I'm eager to return before I go,
For all the pleasures I have known beat thick
On my remembrance. How I long for night!
 That both the sweets of mutual love may try,   460
 And once triumph o'er Caesar ere we die.   *Exeunt.*

---

447. She's] *C1;* She *Q1–3.*   461. ere] *Q2–3,C1; om. Q1.*

433–435. *But . . . behind*] See ll. 387–389, above.

ACT III

At one door enter Cleopatra, Charmion, Iras, *and* Alexas, *a train of Egyptians; at the other,* Antony *and* Romans. *The entrance on both sides is prepared by music, the trumpets first sounding on Antony's part, then answered by timbrels, etc., on Cleopatra's.* Charmion *and* Iras *hold a laurel wreath betwixt them. A dance of Egyptians. After the ceremony,* Cleopatra *crowns* Antony.

ANTONY.
    I thought how those white arms would fold me in,
    And strain me close, and melt me into love;
    So pleased with that sweet image, I sprung forwards,
    And added all my strength to every blow.

CLEOPATRA.
    Come to me, come, my soldier, to my arms!   5
    You've been too long away from my embraces,
    But when I have you fast, and all my own,
    With broken murmurs and with amorous sighs
    I'll say you were unkind, and punish you
    And mark you red with many an eager kiss.   10

ANTONY.
    My brighter Venus!

CLEOPATRA.   O my greater Mars!

ANTONY.
    Thou join'st us well, my love!
    Suppose me come from the Phlegraean plains
    Where gasping giants lay, cleft by my sword,
    And mountain tops pared off each other blow   15
    To bury those I slew. Receive me, goddess!
    Let Caesar spread his subtile nets, like Vulcan;

0.4 *part*] *Q1–2,C1; parts Q3.*   17. subtile] *Q1;* subtle *Q2–3,C1.*

---

13. *Phlegraean plains*] scene of the battle in which the gods, assisted by Hercules, overcame the giants. The defeated giants were believed to be buried under various volcanoes in Greece and Italy.
15. *each other blow*] alternately. One blow slays a giant, the next slices off a mountain top to bury him.
11, 17–23. *Venus . . . Mars . . . Vulcan . . . god*] Learning that his wife Venus was committing adultery with Mars, Vulcan attempted to

– 68 –

In thy embraces I would be beheld
By heav'n and earth at once,
And make their envy what they meant their sport.   20
Let those who took us blush; I would love on
With awful state, regardless of their frowns,
As their superior god.
There's no satiety of love in thee:
Enjoyed, thou still art new; perpetual spring   25
Is in thy arms; the ripened fruit but falls,
And blossoms rise to fill its empty place,
And I grow rich by giving.

Enter Ventidius, *and stands apart.*

ALEXAS.

Oh, now the danger's past, your general comes!
He joins not in your joys, nor minds your triumphs,   30
But with contracted brows looks frowning on,
As envying your success.

ANTONY.

Now, on my soul, he loves me, truly loves me.
He never flattered me in any vice,
But awes me with his virtue. Ev'n this minute,   35
Methinks, he has a right of chiding me.
Lead to the temple: I'll avoid his presence;
It checks too strong upon me.   *Exeunt the rest.*

As Antony *is going,* Ventidius *pulls him by the robe.*

VENTIDIUS.   Emperor!
ANTONY *(looking back).*
'Tis the old argument. I prithee, spare me.

29. comes] *Q1–2,C1;* come *Q3.*

---

punish the two lovers by trapping them in bed in a fine unbreakable
net and then calling in the other gods to laugh. Mercury confessed,
however, that he would gladly change places with Mars *(Odyssey*
VIII.266–366). The comparison of Antony and Cleopatra to Mars and
Venus is a pervasive metaphor in Shakespeare's play.
24–28. *There's . . . giving*] Cf. *Antony and Cleopatra,* II.ii.240–243:
"Age cannot wither her, nor custom stale/ Her infinite variety.
Other women cloy/ The appetites they feed, but she makes hungry/
Where most she satisfies."

VENTIDIUS.

But this one hearing, emperor.

ANTONY.   Let go   40
My robe; or, by my father Hercules—

VENTIDIUS.

By Hercules his father, that's yet greater,
I bring you somewhat you would wish to know.

ANTONY.

Thou see'st we are observed; attend me here,
And I'll return.   *Exit.*   45

VENTIDIUS.

I'm waning in his favor, yet I love him;
I love this man who runs to meet his ruin.
And sure the gods, like me, are fond of him:
His virtues lie so mingled with his crimes,
As would confound their choice to punish one   50
And not reward the other.

Enter Antony.

ANTONY.   We can conquer,
You see, without your aid.
We have dislodged their troops;
They look on us at distance, and like curs
'Scaped from the lion's paws, they bay far off,   55
And lick their wounds, and faintly threaten war.
Five thousand Romans with their faces upward
Lie breathless on the plain.

VENTIDIUS.   'Tis well; and he
Who lost 'em could have spared ten thousand more.
Yet if, by this advantage, you could gain   60
An easier peace, while Caesar doubts the chance
Of arms—

ANTONY.   Oh, think not on't, Ventidius!
The boy pursues my ruin, he'll no peace;
His malice is considerate in advantage.

51. conquer,] *Q2–3,C1;* conquer.   52. aid.] *Q1–2;* aid, *Q3,C1.*
Q1.

42. *Hercules his father*] i.e., Hercules's father, Jupiter.

Oh, he's the coolest murderer! so staunch, 65
He kills, and keeps his temper.
VENTIDIUS.   Have you no friend
  In all his army who has pow'r to move him?
  Maecenas or Agrippa might do much.
ANTONY.
  They're both too deep in Caesar's interests.
  We'll work it out by dint of sword, or perish. 70
VENTIDIUS.
  Fain I would find some other.
ANTONY.   Thank thy love.
  Some four or five such victories as this
  Will save thy farther pains.
VENTIDIUS.
  Expect no more; Caesar is on his guard.
  I know, sir, you have conquered against odds, 75
  But still you draw supplies from one poor town,
  And of Egyptians; he has all the world,
  And at his back nations come pouring in
  To fill the gaps you make. Pray, think again.
ANTONY.
  Why dost thou drive me from myself, to search 80
  For foreign aids? to hunt my memory,
  And range all o'er a waste and barren place
  To find a friend? The wretched have no friends.—
  Yet I had one, the bravest youth of Rome,
  Whom Caesar loves beyond the love of women; 85
  He could resolve his mind as fire does wax,
  From that hard, rugged image melt him down,
  And mold him in what softer form he pleased.
VENTIDIUS.
  Him would I see, that man of all the world;
  Just such a one we want.
ANTONY.   He loved me too: 90
  I was his soul, he lived not but in me.
  We were so closed within each other's breasts,
  The rivets were not found that joined us first.

78. back] *Q1–3;* beck *C1.*

–71–

That does not reach us yet: we were so mixed
As meeting streams, both to ourselves were lost;   95
We were one mass; we could not give or take
But from the same, for he was I, I he.

VENTIDIUS *(aside)*.

He moves as I would wish him.

ANTONY.   After this,
I need not tell his name: 'twas Dolabella.

VENTIDIUS.

He's now in Caesar's camp.

ANTONY.   No matter where,   100
Since he's no longer mine. He took unkindly
That I forbade him Cleopatra's sight
Because I feared he loved her. He confessed
He had a warmth which, for my sake, he stifled;
For 'twere impossible that two, so one,   105
Should not have loved the same. When he departed,
He took no leave, and that confirmed my thoughts.

VENTIDIUS.

It argues that he loved you more than her,
Else he had stayed. But he perceived you jealous,
And would not grieve his friend. I know he loves you.   110

ANTONY.

I should have seen him, then, ere now.

VENTIDIUS.   Perhaps
He has thus long been lab'ring for your peace.

ANTONY.

Would he were here!

VENTIDIUS.   Would you believe he loved you?
I read your answer in your eyes: you would.
Not to conceal it longer, he has sent   115
A messenger from Caesar's camp with letters.

ANTONY.

Let him appear.

VENTIDIUS.   I'll bring him instantly.

Exit Ventidius, *and re-enters immediately with* Dolabella.

111. Perhaps] *Q1–2;* Perhaps.
Q3,C1.

ANTONY.

'Tis he himself! himself, by holy friendship!

Runs to embrace him.

Art thou returned at last, my better half?

Come, give me all myself! —Let me not live,   120

If the young bridegroom, longing for his night,

Was ever half so fond.

DOLABELLA.

I must be silent, for my soul is busy

About a nobler work: she's new come home,

Like a long-absent man, and wanders o'er   125

Each room, a stranger to her own, to look

If all be safe.

ANTONY.   Thou hast what's left of me;

For I am now so sunk from what I was,

Thou find'st me at my lowest watermark.

The rivers that ran in and raised my fortunes   130

Are all dried up, or take another course.

What I have left is from my native spring;

I've still a heart that swells in scorn of fate,

And lifts me to my banks.

DOLABELLA.

Still you are lord of all the world to me.   135

ANTONY.

Why, then I yet am so; for thou art all.

If I had any joy when thou wert absent,

I grudged it to myself; methought I robbed

Thee of thy part. But, O my Dolabella!

Thou hast beheld me other than I am.   140

Hast thou not seen my morning chambers filled

With sceptered slaves who waited to salute me?

With eastern monarchs who forgot the sun

To worship my uprising? Menial kings

Ran coursing up and down my palace-yard,   145

Stood silent in my presence, watched my eyes,

And at my least command all started out

---

120. Come . . . live] *printed as*   124. nobler] *Q1;* noble *Q2–3,C1.*
two separate lines in Q1–3,C1.   145. Ran] *Q1–2;* Run *Q3,C1.*

Like racers to the goal.

DOLABELLA.   Slaves to your fortune.

ANTONY.

Fortune is Caesar's now; and what am I?

VENTIDIUS.

What you have made yourself; I will not flatter.   150

ANTONY.

Is this friendly done?

DOLABELLA.

Yes, when his end is so, I must join with him;
Indeed I must, and yet you must not chide:
Why am I else your friend?

ANTONY.   Take heed, young man,
How thou upbraid'st my love: the queen has eyes,   155
And thou too hast a soul. Canst thou remember
When, swelled with hatred, thou beheld'st her first,
As accessary to thy brother's death?

DOLABELLA.

Spare my remembrance; 'twas a guilty day,
And still the blush hangs here.

ANTONY.   To clear herself   160
For sending him no aid, she came from Egypt.
Her galley down the silver Cydnos rowed,
The tackling silk, the streamers waved with gold;
The gentle winds were lodged in purple sails.
Her nymphs, like Nereids, round her couch were placed, 165
Where she, another sea-born Venus, lay.

DOLABELLA.

No more; I would not hear it.

ANTONY.   Oh, you must!
She lay, and leant her cheek upon her hand,

148. goal] *Q1,Q3,C1;* gaol *Q2.*   166. Where] *Q1–2,C1;* Were *Q3.*

---

158. *thy brother's death*] apparently P. Cornelius Dolabella, who,
besieged by Cassius in the city of Laodicea in 43 B.C., committed
suicide by having a guard cut off his head. In reality, Cleopatra *did*
send him aid.
162–182. *Her galley . . . voice*] This is Dryden's adaptation of Shakespeare's famous description in *Antony and Cleopatra,* II.ii.196–223.
The Cydnus river flowed through the midst of Tarsus.

And cast a look so languishingly sweet
As if, secure of all beholders' hearts,   170
Neglecting she could take 'em. Boys like Cupids
Stood fanning with their painted wings the winds
That played about her face; but if she smiled,
A darting glory seemed to blaze abroad,
That men's desiring eyes were never wearied,   175
But hung upon the object. To soft flutes
The silver oars kept time; and while they played,
The hearing gave new pleasure to the sight,
And both to thought. 'Twas heav'n, or somewhat more;
For she so charmed all hearts, that gazing crowds   180
Stood panting on the shore, and wanted breath
To give their welcome voice.
Then, Dolabella, where was then thy soul?
Was not thy fury quite disarmed with wonder?
Didst thou not shrink behind me from those eyes   185
And whisper in my ear, "Oh, tell her not
That I accused her of my brother's death"?
DOLABELLA.
And should my weakness be a plea for yours?
Mine was an age when love might be excused,
When kindly warmth, and when my springing youth   190
Made it a debt to nature. Yours—
VENTIDIUS.   Speak boldly.
Yours, he would say, in your declining age,
When no more heat was left but what you forced,
When all the sap was needful for the trunk,
When it went down, then you constrained the course,   195
And robbed from nature to supply desire;
In you—I would not use so harsh a word,
But 'tis plain dotage.
ANTONY.   Ha!
DOLABELLA.   'Twas urged too home.

186. ear,] *Q1;* ears? *Q2–3,C1.*   with my brother's death! *Q2–3,*
187. of my brother's death?] *Q1;*   *C1.*
                                    188. for] *Q1,Q3,C1;* fer *Q2.*

198. *home*] near the heart of the matter.

But yet the loss was private that I made;
'Twas but myself I lost. I lost no legions;   200
I had no world to lose, no people's love.

ANTONY.

This from a friend?

DOLABELLA.   Yes, Antony, a true one;
A friend so tender that each word I speak
Stabs my own heart before it reach your ear.
Oh, judge me not less kind because I chide.   205
To Caesar I excuse you.

ANTONY.   O ye gods!
Have I then lived to be excused to Caesar?

DOLABELLA.

As to your equal.

ANTONY.   Well, he's but my equal;
While I wear this, he never shall be more.

DOLABELLA.

I bring conditions from him.

ANTONY.   Are they noble?   210
Methinks thou shouldst not bring 'em else. Yet he
Is full of deep dissembling; knows no honor
Divided from his int'rest. Fate mistook him,
For nature meant him for an usurer:
He's fit indeed to buy, not conquer, kingdoms.   215

VENTIDIUS.

Then, granting this,
What pow'r was theirs who wrought so hard a temper
To honorable terms?

ANTONY.

It was my Dolabella, or some god.

DOLABELLA.

Nor I, nor yet Maecenas nor Agrippa: 220

---

208. ANTONY. Well . . . equal] *Q1;*
om. Q2–3,C1. (This omission
makes l. 209 appear to be as-
signed to Dolabella; hence the
omission of l. 210.S.P. in Q3 and
C1.)

209. be] *Q2–3,C1;* he *Q1.*
210.S.P. DOLABELLA] *Q1–2; om.*
Q3,C1.
220. Nor] *Q1–3;* Not *C1.*
220. nor Agrippa] *Q1–2,C1;* not
Agrippa *Q3.*

---

209. *this*] presumably Antony's sword or his head.

They were your enemies, and I a friend
Too weak alone. Yet 'twas a Roman's deed.
ANTONY.
'Twas like a Roman done. Show me that man
Who has preserved my life, my love, my honor;
Let me but see his face.
VENTIDIUS.   That task is mine,   225
And, heav'n, thou know'st how pleasing.   *Exit* Ventidius.
DOLABELLA.   You'll remember
To whom you stand obliged?
ANTONY.   When I forget it,
Be thou unkind, and that's my greatest curse.
My queen shall thank him too.
DOLABELLA.   I fear she will not.
ANTONY.
But she shall do't—the queen, my Dolabella!   230
Hast thou not still some grudgings of thy fever?
DOLABELLA.
I would not see her lost.
ANTONY.   When I forsake her,
Leave me, my better stars! for she has truth
Beyond her beauty. Caesar tempted her,
At no less price than kingdoms, to betray me,   235
But she resisted all; and yet thou chid'st me
For loving her too well. Could I do so?
DOLABELLA.
Yes; there's my reason.

Re-enter Ventidius *with* Octavia, *leading Antony's two little*
Daughters.

ANTONY.   Where?—Octavia there! *Starting back.*
VENTIDIUS.
What, is she poison to you? a disease?
Look on her, view her well, and those she brings: 240
Are they all strangers to your eyes? has nature
No secret call, no whisper they are yours?

238.S.D. *leading*] *Q1–3; leaving*
C1.

DOLABELLA.

For shame, my lord, if not for love, receive 'em
With kinder eyes. If you confess a man,
Meet 'em, embrace 'em, bid 'em welcome to you.   245
Your arms should open, ev'n without your knowledge,
To clasp 'em in; your feet should turn to wings
To bear you to 'em; and your eyes dart out
And aim a kiss ere you could reach the lips.

ANTONY.

I stood amazed to think how they came hither.   250

VENTIDIUS.

I sent for 'em; I brought 'em in, unknown
To Cleopatra's guards.

DOLABELLA.   Yet are you cold?

OCTAVIA.

Thus long I have attended for my welcome,
Which, as a stranger, sure I might expect.
Who am I?

ANTONY.   Caesar's sister.

OCTAVIA.   That's unkind.   255
Had I been nothing more than Caesar's sister,
Know, I had still remained in Caesar's camp.
But your Octavia, your much injured wife,
Though banished from your bed, driv'n from your house,
In spite of Caesar's sister, still is yours.   260
'Tis true, I have a heart disdains your coldness,
And prompts me not to seek what you should offer;
But a wife's virtue still surmounts that pride.
I come to claim you as my own; to show
My duty first; to ask, nay beg, your kindness.   265
Your hand, my lord: 'tis mine, and I will have it.

Taking his hand.

251. unknown] *Q1–2,C1;* unknow   258. your Octavia] *Q1,C1;* you
Q3.   Octavia *Q2–3.*
253. I have] *Q1–3;* have I *C1.*

244. *confess*] admit you are.
259. *driv'n . . . house*] In 32 B.C., probably at Cleopatra's desire,
Antony ordered Octavia to quit his house in Rome.

VENTIDIUS.

Do, take it; thou deserv'st it.

DOLABELLA.   On my soul,

And so she does. She's neither too submissive,

Nor yet too haughty; but so just a mean

Shows, as it ought, a wife and Roman too.   270

ANTONY.

I fear, Octavia, you have begged my life.

OCTAVIA.

Begged it, my lord?

ANTONY.   Yes, begged it, my ambassadress;

Poorly and basely begged it of your brother.

OCTAVIA.

Poorly and basely I could never beg;

Nor could my brother grant.   275

ANTONY.

Shall I, who to my kneeling slave could say,

"Rise up, and be a king," shall I fall down

And cry, "Forgive me, Caesar"? Shall I set

A man, my equal, in the place of Jove,

As he could give me being? No; that word   280

"Forgive" would choke me up

And die upon my tongue.

DOLABELLA.   You shall not need it.

ANTONY.

I will not need it. Come, you've all betrayed me—

My friend too! —to receive some vile conditions.

My wife has bought me with her prayers and tears,   285

And now I must become her branded slave.

In every peevish mood she will upbraid

The life she gave; if I but look awry,

She cries, "I'll tell my brother."

OCTAVIA.   My hard fortune

Subjects me still to your unkind mistakes.   290

But the conditions I have brought are such

You need not blush to take. I love your honor

---

280. *As*] as if.

Because 'tis mine; it never shall be said
Octavia's husband was her brother's slave.
Sir, you are free—free ev'n from her you loathe.   295
For though my brother bargains for your love,
Makes me the price and cement of your peace,
I have a soul like yours; I cannot take
Your love as alms, nor beg what I deserve.
I'll tell my brother we are reconciled;   300
He shall draw back his troops, and you shall march
To rule the East. I may be dropped at Athens—
No matter where, I never will complain,
But only keep the barren name of wife,
And rid you of the trouble.   305

VENTIDIUS.
Was ever such a strife of sullen honor!
Both scorn to be obliged.

DOLABELLA.
Oh, she has touched him in the tender'st part;
See how he reddens with despite and shame
To be outdone in generosity!   310

VENTIDIUS.
See how he winks! how he dries up a tear
That fain would fall!

ANTONY.
Octavia, I have heard you, and must praise
The greatness of your soul,
But cannot yield to what you have proposed;   315
For I can ne'er be conquered but by love,
And you do all for duty. You would free me,
And would be dropped at Athens; was't not so?

OCTAVIA.
It was, my lord.

ANTONY.   Then I must be obliged
To one who loves me not, who to herself   320
May call me thankless and ungrateful man.
I'll not endure it, no.

307. scorn] *Q1;* scorned *Q2–3,C1.*

-80-

VENTIDIUS.

I'm glad it pinches there.

OCTAVIA.

Would you triumph o'er poor Octavia's virtue?
That pride was all I had to bear me up,   325
That you might think you owed me for your life,
And owed it to my duty, not my love.
I have been injured, and my haughty soul
Could brook but ill the man who slights my bed.

ANTONY.

Therefore you love me not.

OCTAVIA.   Therefore, my lord,   330
I should not love you.

ANTONY.   Therefore you would leave me?

OCTAVIA.

And therefore I should leave you—if I could.

DOLABELLA.

Her soul's too great, after such injuries,
To say she loves; and yet she lets you see it.
Her modesty and silence plead her cause.   335

ANTONY.

O Dolabella, which way shall I turn?
I find a secret yielding in my soul;
But Cleopatra, who would die with me,
Must she be left? Pity pleads for Octavia,
But does it not plead more for Cleopatra?   340

VENTIDIUS.

Justice and pity both plead for Octavia;
For Cleopatra, neither.
One would be ruined with you, but she first
Had ruined you; the other you have ruined,
And yet she would preserve you.   345
In everything their merits are unequal.

ANTONY.

O my distracted soul!

OCTAVIA.   Sweet heav'n compose it!
Come, come, my lord, if I can pardon you,

335. plead] *Q1–2;* pleads *Q3,C1.*

Methinks you should accept it. Look on these:
Are they not yours? Or stand they thus neglected   350
As they are mine? Go to him, children, go;
Kneel to him, take him by the hand, speak to him,
For you may speak and he may own you, too,
Without a blush; and so he cannot all
His children. Go, I say, and pull him to me,   355
And pull him to yourselves from that bad woman.
You, Agrippina, hang upon his arms,
And you, Antonia, clasp about his waist.
If he will shake you off, if he will dash you
Against the pavement, you must bear it, children,   360
For you are mine, and I was born to suffer.
                    Here the Children *go to him, etc.*

VENTIDIUS.
    Was ever sight so moving? Emperor!
DOLABELLA.
    Friend!
OCTAVIA.   Husband!
BOTH CHILDREN.   Father!
ANTONY.   I am vanquished. Take me,
    Octavia; take me, children; share me all.   *Embracing them.*
    I've been a thriftless debtor to your loves,   365
    And run out much, in riot, from your stock,
    But all shall be amended.
OCTAVIA.   O blest hour!
DOLABELLA.
    O happy change!
VENTIDIUS.   My joy stops at my tongue,
    But it has found two channels here for one,
    And bubbles out above.   370
ANTONY *(to* Octavia).
    This is thy triumph. Lead me where thou wilt,
    Ev'n to thy brother's camp.

354–355. *all/ His children*] Antony's children by Cleopatra included
the twins, Alexander Helios and Cleopatra Selene, and another son,
Ptolemy Philadelphos.
366. *run . . . riot*] spent prodigally.

OCTAVIA.   All there are yours.

Enter Alexas *hastily.*

ALEXAS.

The queen, my mistress, sir, and yours—
ANTONY.   'Tis past.—
Octavia, you shall stay this night. Tomorrow
Caesar and we are one.   375
    Exist, leading Octavia; Dolabella *and the* Children *follow.*
VENTIDIUS.

There's news for you! Run, my officious eunuch,
Be sure to be the first; haste forward;
Haste, my dear eunuch, haste!   *Exit.*
ALEXAS.

This downright fighting fool, this thick-skulled hero,
This blunt, unthinking instrument of death,   380
With plain dull virtue has outgone my wit.
Pleasure forsook my earliest infancy;
The luxury of others robbed my cradle,
And ravished thence the promise of a man.
Cast out from nature, disinherited   385
Of what her meanest children claim by kind,
Yet greatness kept me from contempt: that's gone.
Had Cleopatra followed my advice,
Then he had been betrayed who now forsakes.
She dies for love, but she has known its joys.   390
Gods, is this just that I, who know no joys,
Must die because she loves?

    Enter Cleopatra, Charmion, Iras, *train.*

O madam, I have seen what blasts my eyes!
Octavia's here!
CLEOPATRA.   Peace with that raven's note.
I know it too, and now am in   395
The pangs of death.

373–374. 'Tis . . . Tomorrow]   386. children] *Q1–2,C1;* childrem
printed as one line in Q1–3,C1.   *Q3.*
374. you] *Q1,Q3,C1;* yon *Q2.*   387. kept] *Q1–3;* keeps *C1.*
376. my officious eunuch] *printed*   391. know] *Q3–5,C1–2;* knows
as separate line in Q1–3,C1.   *Q1–2.*

ALEXAS.   You are no more a queen;
   Egypt is lost.
CLEOPATRA.   What tell'st thou me of Egypt?
   My life, my soul is lost! Octavia has him,
   O fatal name to Cleopatra's love!
   My kisses, my embraces now are hers,   400
   While I— But thou hast seen my rival. Speak,
   Does she deserve this blessing? Is she fair,
   Bright as a goddess? and is all perfection
   Confined to her? —It is. Poor I was made
   Of that coarse matter which, when she was finished,   405
   The gods threw by for rubbish.
ALEXAS.
   She's indeed a very miracle.
CLEOPATRA.
   Death to my hopes, a miracle!
ALEXAS *(bowing)*.   A miracle—
   I mean, of goodness; for in beauty, madam,
   You make all wonders cease.
CLEOPATRA.   I was too rash.   410
   Take this in part of recompense. But, oh!   *Giving a ring.*
   I fear thou flatter'st me.
CHARMION.
   She comes! she's here!
IRAS.   Fly, madam, Caesar's sister!
CLEOPATRA.
   Were she the sister of the thund'rer Jove,
   And bore her brother's lightning in her eyes,   415
   Thus would I face my rival.

Meets Octavia *with* Ventidius. Octavia *bears up to her. Their
trains come up on either side.*

OCTAVIA.
   I need not ask if you are Cleopatra:
   Your haughty carriage—

411. recompense] *Q1–3;* recem-   414. Were] *Q1–2,C1; Where Q3.*
pence *C1.*   417.S.P. OCTAVIA.] *Q2–3, C1; Oc-*
                                      tab. Q1.

CLEOPATRA.   Shows I am a queen.
  Nor need I ask you who you are.
OCTAVIA.   A Roman:
  A name that makes, and can unmake, a queen.   420
CLEOPATRA.
  Your lord, the man who serves me, is a Roman.
OCTAVIA.
  He was a Roman, till he lost that name
  To be a slave in Egypt; but I come
  To free him thence.
CLEOPATRA.   Peace, peace, my lover's Juno.
  When he grew weary of that household clog,   425
  He chose my easier bonds.
OCTAVIA.   I wonder not
  Your bonds are easy. You have long been practised
  In that lascivious art. He's not the first
  For whom you spread your snares: let Caesar witness.
CLEOPATRA.
  I loved not Caesar; 'twas but gratitude   430
  I paid his love. The worst your malice can
  Is but to say the greatest of mankind
  Has been my slave. The next, but far above him
  In my esteem, is he whom law calls yours,
  But whom his love made mine.
OCTAVIA (coming up close to her). I would view nearer 435
  That face which has so long usurped my right,
  To find th'inevitable charms that catch
  Mankind so sure, that ruined my dear lord.
CLEOPATRA.
  Oh, you do well to search, for had you known
  But half these charms, you had not lost his heart.   440
OCTAVIA.
  Far be their knowledge from a Roman lady,
  Far from a modest wife! Shame of our sex,
  Dost thou not blush to own those black endearments
  That make sin pleasing?
CLEOPATRA.   You may blush, who want 'em.

---

444. want] lack.

If bounteous nature, if indulgent heav'n   445
Have giv'n me charms to please the bravest man,
Should I not thank 'em? Should I be ashamed,
And not be proud? I am, that he has loved me;
And when I love not him, heav'n change this face
For one like that.
OCTAVIA.   Thou lov'st him not so well.   450
CLEOPATRA.
    I love him better, and deserve him more.
OCTAVIA.
    You do not—cannot: you have been his ruin.
    Who made him cheap at Rome, but Cleopatra?
    Who made him scorned abroad, but Cleopatra?
    At Actium, who betrayed him? Cleopatra.   455
    Who made his children orphans, and poor me
    A wretched widow? Only Cleopatra.
CLEOPATRA.
    Yet she who loves him best is Cleopatra.
    If you have suffered, I have suffered more.
    You bear the specious title of a wife   460
    To gild your cause, and draw the pitying world
    To favor it; the world contemns poor me,
    For I have lost my honor, lost my fame,
    And stained the glory of my royal house,
    And all to bear the branded name of mistress.   465
    There wants but life, and that too I would lose
    For him I love.
OCTAVIA.   Be't so, then; take thy wish.   *Exit cum suis.*
CLEOPATRA.
    And 'tis my wish,
    Now he is lost for whom alone I lived.
    My sight grows dim, and every object dances   470
    And swims before me in the maze of death.
    My spirits, while they were opposed, kept up;
    They could not sink beneath a rival's scorn.
    But now she's gone, they faint.

457. widow] *Q1–3;* vidow *C1.*

467.1. *cum suis*] with her train.

ALEXAS.   Mine have had leisure
   To recollect their strength, and furnish counsel   475
   To ruin her who else must ruin you.
CLEOPATRA.   Vain promiser!
   Lead me, my Charmion; nay, your hand too, Iras:
   My grief has weight enough to sink you both.
   Conduct me to some solitary chamber,
   And draw the curtains round;   480
   Then leave me to myself, to take alone
   My fill of grief.
       There I till death will his unkindness weep,
       As harmless infants moan themselves asleep. *Exeunt.*

ACT IV

Antony, Dolabella.

DOLABELLA.
Why would you shift it from yourself on me?
Can you not tell her you must part?
ANTONY.   I cannot.
I could pull out an eye and bid it go,
And t'other should not weep. O Dolabella,
How many deaths are in this word, "Depart"!   5
I dare not trust my tongue to tell her so:
One look of hers would thaw me into tears,
And I should melt till I were lost again.
DOLABELLA.
Then let Ventidius;
He's rough by nature.
ANTONY.   Oh, he'll speak too harshly;   10
He'll kill her with the news. Thou, only thou!
DOLABELLA.
Nature has cast me in so soft a mold
That but to hear a story feigned, for pleasure,
Of some sad lover's death moistens my eyes,
And robs me of my manhood. I should speak   15
So faintly, with such fear to grieve her heart,
She'd not believe it earnest.
ANTONY.   Therefore, therefore
Thou only, thou art fit. Think thyself me,
And when thou speak'st (but let it first be long),
Take off the edge from every sharper sound,   20
And let our parting be as gently made
As other loves begin. Wilt thou do this?
DOLABELLA.
What you have said so sinks into my soul
That if I must speak, I shall speak just so.
ANTONY.
I leave you then to your sad task. Farewell!   25

0.1. Antony] *Q1-2; Enter* Antony
Q3,C1.

– 88 –

I sent her word to meet you.
Goes to the door and comes back.
I forgot.
Let her be told I'll make her peace with mine.
Her crown and dignity shall be preserved,
If I have pow'r with Caesar. —Oh, be sure
To think on that.
DOLABELLA.   Fear not, I will remember.   30
Antony *goes again to the door and comes back.*
ANTONY.

And tell her, too, how much I was constrained;
I did not this but with extremest force.
Desire her not to hate my memory,
For I still cherish hers. —Insist on that.
DOLABELLA.

Trust me, I'll not forget it.
ANTONY.   Then that's all.   35
Goes out and returns again.
Wilt thou forgive my fondness this once more?
Tell her, though we shall never meet again,
If I should hear she took another love,
The news would break my heart. —Now I must go,
For every time I have returned, I feel   40
My soul more tender, and my next command
Would be to bid her stay, and ruin both.   *Exit.*
DOLABELLA.

Men are but children of a larger growth;
Our appetites as apt to change as theirs,
And full as craving too, and full as vain.   45
And yet the soul, shut up in her dark room,
Viewing so clear abroad, at home sees nothing;
But like a mole in earth, busy and blind,
Works all her folly up and casts it outward
To the world's open view. Thus I discovered,   50
And blamed, the love of ruined Antony,
Yet wish that I were he, to be so ruined.

---

44. appetites] *Q1–3;* appetite's *C1.*

Enter Ventidius *above.*

VENTIDIUS.

    Alone? and talking to himself? concerned, too?
    Perhaps my guess is right; he loved her once,
    And may pursue it still.

DOLABELLA.   O friendship! friendship!   55
    Ill canst thou answer this; and reason, worse.
    Unfaithful in th'attempt; hopeless to win;
    And, if I win, undone: mere madness all.
    And yet th'occasion's fair. What injury
    To him, to wear the robe which he throws by?   60

VENTIDIUS.

    None, none at all. This happens as I wish,
    To ruin her yet more with Antony.

Enter Cleopatra, *talking with* Alexas; Charmion, Iras *on the other side.*

DOLABELLA.

    She comes! What charms have sorrow on that face!
    Sorrow seems pleased to dwell with so much sweetness;
    Yet, now and then, a melancholy smile   65
    Breaks loose, like lightning in a winter's night,
    And shows a moment's day.

VENTIDIUS.

    If she should love him too! Her eunuch there!
    That porc'pisce bodes ill weather. Draw, draw nearer,
    Sweet devil, that I may hear.

ALEXAS.   Believe me; try   70

Dolabella *goes over to* Charmion *and* Iras; *seems to talk with them.*

69. That . . . nearer] *Q1–2;*   70.1. Charmion] *Q1–2,C1;* Chari-
printed *as two short lines in*   mon *Q3.*
Q3,C1.

52.1. *above*] on a balcony over one of the doors at the side of the stage.
69. *porc'pisce*] porpoise, popularly thought to be a harbinger of storms.

To make him jealous. Jealousy is like
A polished glass held to the lips when life's in doubt:
If there be breath, 'twill catch the damp, and show it.

CLEOPATRA.

I grant you, jealousy's a proof of love,
But 'tis a weak and unavailing med'cine;   75
It puts out the disease, and makes it show,
But has no pow'r to cure.

ALEXAS.

'Tis your last remedy, and strongest too.
And then this Dolabella—who so fit
To practice on? He's handsome, valiant, young,   80
And looks as he were laid for nature's bait
To catch weak women's eyes.
He stands already more than half suspected
Of loving you. The least kind word or glance
You give this youth will kindle him with love;   85
Then, like a burning vessel set adrift,
You'll send him down amain before the wind
To fire the heart of jealous Antony.

CLEOPATRA.

Can I do this? Ah, no; my love's so true
That I can neither hide it where it is,   90
Nor show it where it is not. Nature meant me
A wife, a silly, harmless, household dove,
Fond without art, and kind without deceit;
But Fortune, that has made a mistress of me,
Has thrust me out to the wide world, unfurnished   95
Of falsehood to be happy.

ALEXAS.   Force yourself.
Th'event will be, your lover will return
Doubly desirous to possess the good
Which once he feared to lose.

95. Has] *Q5,C1–2;* Hast *Q1–4.*

---

72. *A . . . doubt*] a hypermetric line.
76. *puts out*] brings out.
97. *event*] outcome.

CLEOPATRA.   I must attempt it;
    But oh, with what regret!   *Exit* Alexas. 100

            She comes up to Dolabella.

VENTIDIUS.
    So, now the scene draws near; they're in my reach.
CLEOPATRA *(to* Dolabella).
    Discoursing with my women! Might not I
    Share in your entertainment?
CHARMION.   You have been
    The subject of it, madam.
CLEOPATRA.   How! and how?
IRAS.
    Such praises of your beauty!
CLEOPATRA.   Mere poetry.   105
    Your Roman wits, your Gallus and Tibullus,
    Have taught you this from Cytheris and Delia.
DOLABELLA.
    Those Roman wits have never been in Egypt;
    Cytheris and Delia else had been unsung.
    I, who have seen—had I been born a poet,   110
    Should choose a nobler name.
CLEOPATRA.   You flatter me.
    But 'tis your nation's vice: all of your country
    Are flatt'rers, and all false. Your friend's like you.
    I'm sure he sent you not to speak these words.
DOLABELLA.
    No, madam; yet he sent me—
CLEOPATRA.   Well, he sent you—   115
DOLABELLA.
    Of a less pleasing errand.

101. near;] *Q1–2;* near, *Q3,C1.*

---

106. *Gallus and Tibullus*] Gaius Cornelius Gallus (69?–26 B.C.), co-incidentally one of Octavius's commanders in the war against Antony and Cleopatra, wrote love poems about the actress Cytheris. Albius Tibullus (48?–19 B.C.) celebrated a woman he called Delia in his elegies.

CLEOPATRA.   How less pleasing?
    Less to yourself, or me?
DOLABELLA.   Madam, to both;
    For you must mourn, and I must grieve to cause it.
CLEOPATRA.
    You, Charmion, and your fellow, stand at distance.—
    (Aside.) Hold up, my spirits. —Well, now your mournful
                                                    matter; 120
    For I'm prepared, perhaps can guess it too.
DOLABELLA.
    I wish you would, for 'tis a thankless office
    To tell ill news; and I, of all your sex,
    Most fear displeasing you.
CLEOPATRA.   Of all your sex,
    I soonest could forgive you, if you should.   125
VENTIDIUS.
    Most delicate advances! Woman! Woman!
    Dear, damned, inconstant sex!
CLEOPATRA.   In the first place,
    I am to be forsaken. Is't not so?
DOLABELLA.
    I wish I could not answer to that question.
CLEOPATRA.
    Then pass it o'er because it troubles you: 130
    I should have been more grieved another time.
    Next, I'm to lose my kingdom. —Farewell, Egypt!
    Yet, is there any more?
DOLABELLA.   Madam, I fear
    Your too deep sense of grief has turned your reason.
CLEOPATRA.
    No, no, I'm not run mad. I can bear fortune,   135
    And love may be expelled by other love,
    As poisons are by poisons.
DOLABELLA.
    You o'erjoy me, madam,
    To find your griefs so moderately borne.
    You've heard the worst; all are not false like him.   140

117. yourself] *Q1,Q3,C1;* you self
Q2.

CLEOPATRA.

No; heav'n forbid they should.

DOLABELLA.   Some men are constant.

CLEOPATRA.

And constancy deserves reward, that's certain.

DOLABELLA.

Deserves it not; but give it leave to hope.

VENTIDIUS.

I'll swear thou hast my leave. I have enough.
But how to manage this! Well, I'll consider.   *Exit.* 145

DOLABELLA.

I came prepared
To tell you heavy news—news which, I thought,
Would fright the blood from your pale cheeks to hear.
But you have met it with a cheerfulness
That makes my task more easy; and my tongue,   150
Which on another's message was employed,
Would gladly speak its own.

CLEOPATRA.   Hold, Dolabella.
First tell me, were you chosen by my lord,
Or sought you this employment?

DOLABELLA.

He picked me out, and as his bosom friend,   155
He charged me with his words.

CLEOPATRA.   The message then
I know was tender, and each accent smooth,
To mollify that rugged word, "Depart."

DOLABELLA.

Oh, you mistake. He chose the harshest words;
With fiery eyes and with contracted brows,   160
He coined his face in the severest stamp,
And fury shook his fabric like an earthquake.
He heaved for vent, and burst like bellowing Aetna
In sounds scarce human, "Hence, away forever;
Let her begone, the blot of my renown,   165
And bane of all my hopes!

All the time of this speech, Cleopatra *seems more and more con-cerned, till she sinks quite down.*

Let her be driv'n as far as men can think
From man's commerce! She'll poison to the center!"
CLEOPATRA.
   Oh, I can bear no more!
DOLABELLA.
   Help, help! —O wretch! O cursed, cursed wretch!   170
What have I done!
CHARMION.   Help, chafe her temples, Iras.
IRAS.
   Bend, bend her forward quickly.
CHARMION.   Heav'n be praised,
She comes again.
CLEOPATRA.   Oh, let him not approach me.
Why have you brought me back to this loathed being,
Th'abode of falsehood, violated vows,   175
And injured love? For pity, let me go;
For if there be a place of long repose,
I'm sure I want it. My disdainful lord
Can never break that quiet, nor awake
The sleeping soul with hollowing in my tomb   180
Such words as fright her hence. Unkind, unkind!
DOLABELLA *(kneeling)*.
   Believe me, 'tis against myself I speak;
That sure deserves belief. I injured him:
My friend ne'er spoke those words. Oh, had you seen
How often he came back, and every time   185
With something more obliging and more kind
To add to what he said. What dear farewells!
How almost vanquished by his love he parted,
And leaned to what unwillingly he left!
I, traitor as I was, for love of you   190
(But what can you not do, who made me false?)
I forged that lie; for whose forgiveness kneels
This self-accused, self-punished criminal.
CLEOPATRA.
   With how much ease believe we what we wish!
Rise, Dolabella. If you have been guilty,   195
I have contributed, and too much love
Has made me guilty too.

Th'advance of kindness which I made was feigned
To call back fleeting love by jealousy,
But 'twould not last. Oh, rather let me lose   200
Than so ignobly trifle with his heart.

DOLABELLA.

I find your breast fenced round from human reach,
Transparent as a rock of solid crystal,
Seen through, but never pierced. My friend, my friend!
What endless treasure hast thou thrown away,   205
And scattered, like an infant, in the ocean,
Vain sums of wealth which none can gather thence!

CLEOPATRA.

Could you not beg
An hour's admittance to his private ear?
Like one who wanders through long barren wilds,   210
And yet foreknows no hospitable inn
Is near to succor hunger, eats his fill
Before his painful march:
So would I feed a while my famished eyes
Before we part, for I have far to go,   215
If death be far, and never must return.

              Ventidius *with* Octavia, *behind.*

VENTIDIUS.

From hence you may discover— Oh, sweet, sweet!
Would you indeed? the pretty hand in earnest?

DOLABELLA *(takes her hand).*

I will, for this reward. —Draw it not back,
'Tis all I e'er will beg.   220

VENTIDIUS.

They turn upon us.

OCTAVIA.   What quick eyes has guilt!

VENTIDIUS.

Seem not to have observed 'em, and go on.

---

212. eats his fill] *printed as the*   219.S.D. *takes her hand]* *placed at*
beginning of l. 213 in Q1–3,C1.   *end of l. 218 in Q1–3,C1.*

216.1. *behind]* at the back of the stage, near the scenery.

They enter.

DOLABELLA.

   Saw you the emperor, Ventidius?

VENTIDIUS.   No.

   I sought him, but I heard that he was private,

   None with him but Hipparchus, his freedman.   225

DOLABELLA.

   Know you his business?

VENTIDIUS.   Giving him instructions

   And letters to his brother Caesar.

DOLABELLA.   Well,

   He must be found.   *Exeunt* Dolabella *and* Cleopatra.

OCTAVIA.   Most glorious impudence!

VENTIDIUS.

   She looked, methought,

   As she would say, "Take your old man, Octavia;   230

   Thank you, I'm better here." Well, but what use

   Make we of this discovery?

OCTAVIA.   Let it die.

VENTIDIUS.

   I pity Dolabella, but she's dangerous.

   Her eyes have pow'r beyond Thessalian charms

   To draw the moon from heav'n. For eloquence,   235

   The sea-green Sirens taught her voice their flatt'ry,

   And while she speaks, night steals upon the day,

   Unmarked of those that hear. Then she's so charming

   Age buds at sight of her, and swells to youth.

   The holy priests gaze on her when she smiles,   240

   And with heaved hands, forgetting gravity,

   They bless her wanton eyes. Ev'n I, who hate her,

   With a malignant joy behold such beauty,

231. Well . . . use] *printed as a
separate short line in Q1–3,C1.*

---

234. *Thessalian charms*] In the ancient world, Thessaly was a center of
sorcery and enchantment.
240–242. *The . . . eyes*] based on *Antony and Cleopatra,* II.ii.243–245:
". . . for vilest things/ Become themselves in her, that the holy
priests/ Bless her when she is riggish."

And while I curse, desire it. Antony
Must needs have some remains of passion still,   245
Which may ferment into a worse relapse
If now not fully cured. I know, this minute,
With Caesar he's endeavoring her peace.

OCTAVIA.
You have prevailed. —But for a farther purpose   *Walks off.*
I'll prove how he will relish this discovery.   250
What, make a strumpet's peace! it swells my heart;
It must not, sha' not be.

VENTIDIUS.   His guards appear.
Let me begin, and you shall second me.

Enter Antony.

ANTONY.
Octavia, I was looking you, my love.
What, are your letters ready? I have giv'n   255
My last instructions.

OCTAVIA.   Mine, my lord, are written.

ANTONY.
Ventidius!   *Drawing him aside.*

VENTIDIUS.   My lord?

ANTONY.   A word in private.—
When saw you Dolabella?

VENTIDIUS.   Now, my lord,
He parted hence, and Cleopatra with him.

ANTONY.
Speak softly. —'Twas by my command he went,   260
To bear my last farewell.

VENTIDIUS *(aloud).*   It looked indeed
Like your farewell.

ANTONY.   More softly. —My farewell?
What secret meaning have you in those words
Of "my farewell"? He did it by my order.

VENTIDIUS *(aloud).*
Then he obeyed your order. I suppose   265
You bid him do it with all gentleness,
All kindness, and all—love.

ANTONY.   How she mourned,
The poor forsaken creature!

VENTIDIUS.

She took it as she ought; she bore your parting
As she did Caesar's, as she would another's   270
Were a new love to come.

ANTONY *(aloud)*.   Thou dost belie her;
Most basely and maliciously belie her.

VENTIDIUS.

I thought not to displease you; I have done.

OCTAVIA *(coming up)*.
You seem disturbed, my lord.

ANTONY.   A very trifle.
Retire, my love.

VENTIDIUS.   It was indeed a trifle.   275
He sent—

ANTONY *(angrily)*. No more. Look how thou disobey'st me;
Thy life shall answer it.

OCTAVIA.   Then 'tis no trifle.

VENTIDIUS *(to* Octavia).
'Tis less, a very nothing. You too saw it,
As well as I, and therefore 'tis no secret.

ANTONY.
She saw it!

VENTIDIUS.   Yes. She saw young Dolabella—   280

ANTONY.
Young Dolabella!

VENTIDIUS.   Young, I think him young,
And handsome too, and so do others think him.
But what of that? He went by your command,
Indeed 'tis probable, with some kind message,
For she received it graciously. She smiled,   285
And then he grew familiar with her hand,
Squeezed it, and worried it with ravenous kisses.
She blushed, and sighed, and smiled, and blushed again.
At last she took occasion to talk softly,
And brought her cheek up close, and leaned on his;   290
At which, he whispered kisses back on hers,

And then she cried aloud that "constancy
Should be rewarded."

OCTAVIA.   This I saw and heard.

ANTONY.

What woman was it, whom you heard and saw
So playful with my friend? Not Cleopatra?   295

VENTIDIUS.

Ev'n she, my lord.

ANTONY.   My Cleopatra?

VENTIDIUS.

Your Cleopatra;
Dolabella's Cleopatra;
Every man's Cleopatra.

ANTONY.

Thou li'st.

VENTIDIUS.   I do not lie, my lord.   300

Is this so strange? Should mistresses be left,
And not provide against a time of change?
You know she's not much used to lonely nights.

ANTONY.

I'll think no more on't.
I know 'tis false, and see the plot betwixt you.   305
You needed not have gone this way, Octavia.
What harms it you that Cleopatra's just?
She's mine no more. I see, and I forgive;
Urge it no farther, love.

OCTAVIA.   Are you concerned
That she's found false?

ANTONY.   I should be, were it so;   310
For though 'tis past, I would not that the world
Should tax my former choice, that I loved one
Of so light note. But I forgive you both.

294. woman] *Q1,Q3,C1*; womam   300. Thou] *Q1,Q3,C1*; Tou *Q2*.
Q2.   308. more.] *Q1–2*; more, *Q3,C1*.
295. Not Cleopatra?] *printed as a*
separate short line in Q1–3,C1.

297–299. *Your . . . man's Cleopatra*] echoes *Much Ado About Nothing*,
III.ii: "Leonato's Hero, your Hero, every man's Hero."

VENTIDIUS.

    What has my age deserved, that you should think
    I would abuse your ears with perjury?   315
    If heav'n be true, she's false.

ANTONY.   Though heav'n and earth
    Should witness it, I'll not believe her tainted.

VENTIDIUS.

    I'll bring you, then, a witness
    From hell to prove her so.
              Seeing Alexas *just entering, and starting back.*
                  Nay, go not back;
    For stay you must, and shall.

ALEXAS.   What means my lord?   320

VENTIDIUS.

    To make you do what most you hate: speak truth.
    You are of Cleopatra's private counsel,
    Of her bed-counsel, her lascivious hours;
    Are conscious of each nightly change she makes,
    And watch her, as Chaldeans do the moon;   325
    Can tell what signs she passes through, what day.

ALEXAS.

    My noble lord!

VENTIDIUS.   My most illustrious pander,
    No fine set speech, no cadence, no turned periods,
    But a plain homespun truth is what I ask.
    I did myself o'erhear your queen make love   330
    To Dolabella. Speak; for I will know,
    By your confession, what more passed betwixt 'em:
    How near the business draws to your employment,
    And when the happy hour.

ANTONY.

    Speak truth, Alexas. Whether it offend   335
    Or please Ventidius, care not; justify
    Thy injured queen from malice; dare his worst.

319. not] *Q1-2; om. Q3,C1.*   328. no turned] *Q1,Q3,C1;* to
                                           turned *Q2.*

---

325. *Chaldeans*] famed in the ancient world as astronomers and
astrologers.

OCTAVIA *(aside).*

See how he gives him courage! how he fears
To find her false, and shuts his eyes to truth,
Willing to be misled!   340

ALEXAS.

As far as love may plead for woman's frailty,
Urged by desert and greatness of the lover,
So far, divine Octavia, may my queen
Stand ev'n excused to you for loving him
Who is your lord; so far, from brave Ventidius,   345
May her past actions hope a fair report.

ANTONY.

'Tis well and truly spoken. Mark, Ventidius.

ALEXAS.

To you, most noble emp'ror, her strong passion
Stands not excused, but wholly justified.
Her beauty's charms alone, without her crown,   350
From Ind and Meroë drew the distant vows
Of sighing kings, and at her feet were laid
The scepters of the earth, exposed on heaps,
To choose where she would reign.
She thought a Roman only could deserve her,   355
And of all Romans, only Antony;
And, to be less than wife to you, disdained
Their lawful passion.

ANTONY.   'Tis but truth.

ALEXAS.

And yet, though love and your unmatched desert
Have drawn her from the due regard of honor,   360
At last heav'n opened her unwilling eyes
To see the wrongs she offered fair Octavia,
Whose holy bed she lawlessly usurped.
The sad effects of this improsperous war
Confirmed those pious thoughts.

356. Romans] *Q1–2;* Roman *Q3,*   363. lawlessly] *Q1;* lawfully *Q2–3,*
C1.   *C1.*

351. *Meroë*] an island in the Nile, the ancient capital of Ethiopia.

VENTIDIUS *(aside)*.   Oh, wheel you there?   365
  Observe him now; the man begins to mend,
  And talk substantial reason. —Fear not, eunuch;
  The emperor has giv'n thee leave to speak.
ALEXAS.

  Else had I never dared t'offend his ears
  With what the last necessity has urged   370
  On my forsaken mistress; yet I must not
  Presume to say her heart is wholly altered.
ANTONY.

  No, dare not for thy life, I charge thee dare not
  Pronounce that fatal word!
OCTAVIA *(aside)*.

  Must I bear this? Good heav'n, afford me patience.   375
VENTIDIUS.

  On, sweet eunuch; my dear half-man, proceed.
ALEXAS.

  Yet Dolabella
  Has loved her long. He, next my godlike lord,
  Deserves her best; and should she meet his passion,
  Rejected as she is by him she loved—   380
ANTONY.

  Hence from my sight! for I can bear no more.
  Let Furies drag thee quick to hell; let all
  The longer damned have rest; each torturing hand
  Do thou employ, till Cleopatra comes;
  Then join thou too, and help to torture her!   385
                  Exit Alexas, *thrust out by* Antony.
OCTAVIA.

  'Tis not well;
  Indeed, my lord, 'tis much unkind to me
  To show this passion, this extreme concernment
  For an abandoned, faithless prostitute.
ANTONY.

  Octavia, leave me. I am much disordered.   390
  Leave me, I say.

373. thee dare not] *C1;* thee dare   382–383. let . . . rest] *Q1; om.*
not, *Q1–2;* thee dare not. *Q3.*   *Q2–3,C1.*

OCTAVIA.   My lord?
ANTONY.   I bid you leave me.
VENTIDIUS.
      Obey him, madam. Best withdraw a while,
      And see how this will work.
OCTAVIA.
      Wherein have I offended you, my lord,
      That I am bid to leave you? Am I false   395
      Or infamous? Am I a Cleopatra?
      Were I she,
      Base as she is, you would not bid me leave you,
      But hang upon my neck, take slight excuses,
      And fawn upon my falsehood.
ANTONY.   'Tis too much,   400
      Too much, Octavia. I am pressed with sorrows
      Too heavy to be borne, and you add more.
      I would retire, and recollect what's left
      Of man within, to aid me.
OCTAVIA.   You would mourn
      In private for your love, who has betrayed you. 405
      You did but half return to me: your kindness
      Lingered behind with her. I hear, my lord,
      You make conditions for her,
      And would include her treaty. Wondrous proofs
      Of love to me!
ANTONY.   Are you my friend, Ventidius?   410
      Or are you turned a Dolabella too,
      And let this Fury loose?
VENTIDIUS.   Oh, be advised,
      Sweet madam, and retire.
OCTAVIA.
      Yes, I will go, but never to return.
      You shall no more be haunted with this Fury.   415
      My lord, my lord, love will not always last
      When urged with long unkindness and disdain.
      Take her again whom you prefer to me:
      She stays but to be called. Poor cozened man!

418. prefer] *Q1,C1;* perfer *Q2–3.*

Let a feigned parting give her back your heart,   420
Which a feigned love first got. For injured me,
Though my just sense of wrongs forbid my stay,
My duty shall be yours.
To the dear pledges of our former love
My tenderness and care shall be transferred,   425
And they shall cheer, by turns, my widowed nights.
So, take my last farewell, for I despair
To have you whole, and scorn to take you half.   *Exit.*
VENTIDIUS.
I combat heav'n, which blasts my best designs:
My last attempt must be to win her back,   430
But oh! I fear, in vain.   *Exit.*
ANTONY.
Why was I framed with this plain, honest heart,
Which knows not to disguise its griefs and weakness,
But bears its workings outward to the world?
I should have kept the mighty anguish in,   435
And forced a smile at Cleopatra's falsehood.
Octavia had believed it, and had stayed.
But I am made a shallow-forded stream,
Seen to the bottom; all my clearness scorned,
And all my faults exposed. —See where he comes   440

               Enter Dolabella.

Who has profaned the sacred name of friend,
And worn it into vileness!
With how secure a brow, and specious form,
He gilds the secret villain! Sure that face
Was meant for honesty, but heav'n mismatched it,   445
And furnished treason out with nature's pomp
To make its work more easy.
DOLABELLA.   O my friend!

422. my   stay]   *Q1–2*   me   stay
Q3,C1.

432–440. *Why . . . exposed*] Plutarch emphasizes that Antony "was a
plain man without subtlety."

ANTONY.

Well, Dolabella, you performed my message?

DOLABELLA.

I did, unwillingly.

ANTONY.   Unwillingly?

Was it so hard for you to bear our parting?   450
You should have wished it.

DOLABELLA.   Why?

ANTONY.   Because you love me.

And she received my message with as true,
With as unfeigned a sorrow as you brought it?

DOLABELLA.

She loves you, ev'n to madness.

ANTONY.   Oh, I know it.

You, Dolabella, do not better know   455
How much she loves me. And should I
Forsake this beauty, this all-perfect creature?

DOLABELLA.

I could not, were she mine.

ANTONY.   And yet you first

Persuaded me. How come you altered since?

DOLABELLA.

I said at first I was not fit to go: 460
I could not hear her sighs, and see her tears,
But pity must prevail. And so perhaps
It may again with you, for I have promised
That she should take her last farewell; and see,
She comes to claim my word.

Enter Cleopatra.

ANTONY.   False Dolabella!   465

DOLABELLA.

What's false, my lord?

ANTONY.   Why, Dolabella's false,

And Cleopatra's false; both false and faithless.
Draw near, you well-joined wickedness, you serpents

---

468. *serpents*] The story of the bosom serpent is a proverbial illustra-
tion of ingratitude and treachery. The tradition may originate in
Aesop, *Fables*, I.x.

Whom I have in my kindly bosom warmed
Till I am stung to death.
DOLABELLA.   My lord, have I   470
Deserved to be thus used?
CLEOPATRA.   Can heav'n prepare
A newer torment? Can it find a curse
Beyond our separation?
ANTONY.   Yes, if fate
Be just, much greater: heav'n should be ingenious
In punishing such crimes. The rolling stone   475
And gnawing vulture were slight pains, invented
When Jove was young, and no examples known
Of mighty ills; but you have ripened sin
To such a monstrous growth, 'twill pose the gods
To find an equal torture. Two, two such—   480
Oh, there's no farther name! two such—to me,
To me who locked my soul within your breasts,
Had no desires, no joys, no life, but you.
When half the globe was mine, I gave it you
In dowry with my heart; I had no use,   485
No fruit of all, but you; a friend and mistress
Was what the world could give. O Cleopatra!
O Dolabella! how could you betray
This tender heart, which with an infant fondness
Lay lulled betwixt your bosoms, and there slept   490
Secure of injured faith?
DOLABELLA.   If she has wronged you,
Heav'n, hell, and you revenge it.
ANTONY.   If she wronged me!
Thou wouldst evade thy part of guilt; but swear
Thou lov'st not her.

469. warmed] *Q1,Q3,C1;* warm'   476. were] *Q1,Q3,C1;* we *Q2.*
Q2.

475–476. *rolling stone . . . gnawing vulture*] In Hades, Sisyphus was
doomed eternally to roll uphill a heavy stone, which always rolled
down again. Tityus was tortured by having vultures gnaw perpetually
at his liver.
479. *pose*] puzzle.
491. *Secure of*] safe from.

DOLABELLA.   Not so as I love you.

ANTONY.

    Not so? Swear, swear, I say, thou dost not love her.   495

DOLABELLA.

    No more than friendship will allow.

ANTONY.   No more?

    Friendship allows thee nothing: thou art perjured.—
    And yet thou didst not swear thou lov'dst her not,
    But not so much, no more. O trifling hypocrite,
    Who dar'st not own to her thou dost not love,   500
    Nor own to me thou dost! Ventidius heard it;
    Octavia saw it.

CLEOPATRA.   They are enemies.

ANTONY.

    Alexas is not so. He, he confessed it;
    He who, next hell, best knew it, he avowed it.
    (To Dolabella.)   Why do I seek a proof beyond yourself?   505
    You, whom I sent to bear my last farewell,
    Returned to plead her stay.

DOLABELLA.   What shall I answer?

    If to have loved be guilt, then I have sinned;
    But if to have repented of that love
    Can wash away my crime, I have repented.   510
    Yet, if I have offended past forgiveness,
    Let not her suffer: she is innocent.

CLEOPATRA.

    Ah, what will not a woman do who loves!
    What means will she refuse to keep that heart
    Where all her joys are placed? 'Twas I encouraged,   515
    'Twas I blew up the fire that scorched his soul,
    To make you jealous, and by that regain you.
    But all in vain: I could not counterfeit;
    In spite of all the dams, my love broke o'er
    And drowned my heart again. Fate took th'occasion,   520
    And thus one minute's feigning has destroyed
    My whole life's truth.

ANTONY.   Thin cobwebs arts of falsehood,

    Seen and broke through at first.

DOLABELLA.   Forgive your mistress.

CLEOPATRA.
Forgive your friend.
ANTONY. You have convinced yourselves;
You plead each other's cause. What witness have you 525
That you but meant to raise my jealousy?
CLEOPATRA.
Ourselves, and heav'n.
ANTONY.
Guilt witnesses for guilt. Hence, love and friendship!
You have no longer place in human breasts;
These two have driv'n you out. Avoid my sight! 530
I would not kill the man whom I have loved,
And cannot hurt the woman; but avoid me.
I do not know how long I can be tame,
For if I stay one minute more to think
How I am wronged, my justice and revenge 535
Will cry so loud within me that my pity
Will not be heard for either.
DOLABELLA. Heav'n has but
Our sorrow for our sins, and then delights
To pardon erring man. Sweet mercy seems
Its darling attribute, which limits justice, 540
As if there were degrees in infinite,
And infinite would rather want perfection
Than punish to extent.
ANTONY. I can forgive
A foe, but not a mistress and a friend.
Treason is there in its most horrid shape 545
Where trust is greatest, and the soul resigned
Is stabbed by its own guards. I'll hear no more;
Hence from my sight forever!
CLEOPATRA. How? Forever?
I cannot go one moment from your sight,
And must I go forever? 550

524. your] *Q1,Q3,C1;* you *Q2*   531. have] *C2; om. Q1–4,C1.*

524. *convinced*] convicted.
530. *Avoid*] leave.

My joys, my only joys, are centered here.
What place have I to go to? My own kingdom?
That I have lost for you. Or to the Romans?
They hate me for your sake. Or must I wander
The wide world o'er, a helpless, banished woman,   555
Banished for love of you—banished from you?
Aye, there's the banishment! Oh, hear me, hear me
With strictest justice, for I beg no favor,
And if I have offended you, then kill me,
But do not banish me.
ANTONY.   I must not hear you.   560
I have a fool within me takes your part,
But honor stops my ears.
CLEOPATRA.   For pity hear me!
Would you cast off a slave who followed you,
Who crouched beneath your spurn? —He has no pity!
See if he gives one tear to my departure,   565
One look, one kind farewell. O iron heart!
Let all the gods look down, and judge betwixt us
If he did ever love!
ANTONY.   No more. —Alexas!
DOLABELLA.
A perjured villain!
ANTONY (to Cleopatra). Your Alexas, yours.
CLEOPATRA.
Oh, 'twas his plot, his ruinous design,   570
T'engage you in my love by jealousy.
Hear him; confront him with me; let him speak.
ANTONY.
I have, I have.
CLEOPATRA.   And if he clear me not—
ANTONY.
Your creature! one who hangs upon your smiles,
Watches your eye to say or to unsay   575
Whate'er you please! I am not to be moved.

---

564. *spurn*] literally, a kick.

CLEOPATRA.

Then must we part? Farewell, my cruel lord!
Th'appearance is against me, and I go,
Unjustified, forever from your sight.
How I have loved, you know; how yet I love,   580
My only comfort is, I know myself.
I love you more, ev'n now you are unkind,
Than when you loved me most; so well, so truly,
I'll never strive against it, but die pleased
To think you once were mine.   585

ANTONY.

Good heav'n, they weep at parting!
Must I weep too? That calls 'em innocent.
I must not weep; and yet I must, to think
That I must not forgive.—
Live, but live wretched; 'tis but just you should,   590
Who made me so. Live from each other's sight;
Let me not hear you meet; set all the earth
And all the seas betwixt your sundered loves;
View nothing common but the sun and skies.
Now, all take several ways,   595
    And each your own sad fate, with mine, deplore:
    That you were false, and I could trust no more.

                          Exeunt severally.

ACT V

Cleopatra, Charmion, Iras.

CHARMION.

Be juster, heav'n: such virtue punished thus
Will make us think that chance rules all above,
And shuffles with a random hand the lots
Which man is forced to draw.

CLEOPATRA.

I could tear out these eyes, that gained his heart   5
And had not pow'r to keep it. O the curse
Of doting on, ev'n when I find it dotage!
Bear witness, gods, you heard him bid me go;
You, whom he mocked with imprecating vows
Of promised faith. —I'll die! I will not bear it.   10
You may hold me—

She pulls out her dagger, and they hold her.

But I can keep my breath; I can die inward,
And choke this love.

Enter Alexas.

IRAS.   Help, O Alexas, help!
The queen grows desperate; her soul struggles in her
With all the agonies of love and rage,   15
And strives to force its passage.

CLEOPATRA.   Let me go.
Art thou there, traitor! —Oh,
Oh, for a little breath, to vent my rage!
Give, give me way, and let me loose upon him.

ALEXAS.

Yes, I deserve it, for my ill-timed truth.   20
Was it for me to prop
The ruins of a falling majesty?
To place myself beneath the mighty flaw,

0.1. Cleopatra] *Q1–2; Enter* Cleopatra *Q3,C1.*

---

12. *keep*] hold.

– 112 –

Thus to be crushed and pounded into atoms
By its o'erwhelming weight? 'Tis too presuming   25
For subjects to preserve that willful pow'r
Which courts its own destruction.
CLEOPATRA.   I would reason
More calmly with you. Did not you o'errule
And force my plain, direct, and open love
Into these crooked paths of jealousy?   30
Now, what's th'event? Octavia is removed,
But Cleopatra's banished. Thou, thou villain,
Hast pushed my boat to open sea, to prove,
At my sad cost, if thou canst steer it back.
It cannot be; I'm lost too far; I'm ruined.   35
Hence, thou imposter, traitor, monster, devil!—
I can no more: thou, and my griefs, have sunk
Me down so low that I want voice to curse thee.
ALEXAS.
Suppose some shipwrecked seaman near the shore,
Dropping and faint with climbing up the cliff;   40
If, from above, some charitable hand
Pull him to safety, hazarding himself
To draw the other's weight, would he look back
And curse him for his pains? The case is yours:
But one step more, and you have gained the height.   45
CLEOPATRA.
Sunk, never more to rise.
ALEXAS.
Octavia's gone, and Dolabella banished.
Believe me, madam, Antony is yours.
His heart was never lost, but started off
To jealousy, love's last retreat and covert,   50
Where it lies hid in shades, watchful in silence,
And list'ning for the sound that calls it back.
Some other, any man ('tis so advanced),
May perfect this unfinished work, which I

33. Hast] *Q5,C2;* Has *Q1–4,C1.*   39. some] *Q1;* from *Q2–3,C1.*

---

31. *event*] outcome.

(Unhappy only to myself) have left   55
So easy to his hand.

CLEOPATRA.   Look well thou do't; else—

ALEXAS.

Else what your silence threatens. —Antony
Is mounted up the Pharos, from whose turret
He stands surveying our Egyptian galleys
Engaged with Caesar's fleet. Now death or conquest!   60
If the first happen, fate acquits my promise;
If we o'ercome, the conqueror is yours.

              A distant shout within.

CHARMION.

Have comfort, madam: did you mark that shout?

              Second shout nearer.

IRAS.

Hark! they redouble it.

ALEXAS.   'Tis from the port.
The loudness shows it near: good news, kind heav'ns!   65

CLEOPATRA.

Osiris make it so!

           Enter Serapion.

SERAPION.   Where, where's the queen?

ALEXAS.

How frightfully the holy coward stares!
As if not yet recovered of th'assault,
When all his gods, and what's more dear to him,
His off'rings, were at stake.

SERAPION.   O horror, horror!   70
Egypt has been; our latest hour is come;
The queen of nations from her ancient seat
Is sunk forever in the dark abyss;
Time has unrolled her glories to the last,
And now closed up the volume.

CLEOPATRA.   Be more plain.   75

---

58. *Pharos*] the lighthouse at Alexandria.
70–73. *O horror . . . abyss*] recalls *Aeneid* II.324–326, which describes
the fall of Troy.

Say whence thou com'st—though fate is in thy face,
Which from thy haggard eyes looks wildly out
And threatens ere thou speak'st.

SERAPION.   I came from Pharos;
From viewing (spare me, and imagine it)
Our land's last hope, your navy—

CLEOPATRA.   Vanquished?

SERAPION.   No.   80
They fought not.

CLEOPATRA.   Then they fled?

SERAPION.   Nor that. I saw,
With Antony, your well-appointed fleet
Row out; and thrice he waved his hand on high,
And thrice with cheerful cries they shouted back.
'Twas then false Fortune, like a fawning strumpet   85
About to leave the bankrupt prodigal,
With a dissembled smile would kiss at parting
And flatter to the last. The well-timed oars
Now dipped from every bank, now smoothly run
To meet the foe; and soon indeed they met,   90
But not as foes. In few, we saw their caps
On either side thrown up; th'Egyptian galleys,
Received like friends, passed through and fell behind
The Roman rear; and now they all come forward,
And ride within the port.

CLEOPATRA.   Enough, Serapion: 95
I've heard my doom. —This needed not, you gods.
When I lost Antony, your work was done;
'Tis but superfluous malice. —Where's my lord?
How bears he this last blow?

SERAPION.
His fury cannot be expressed by words.   100
Thrice he attempted headlong to have fall'n

86. the] *Q1–3;* a *C1.*   87. dissembled] *Q1;* dissembling
                                      Q2–3,C1.

---

91. *In few*] briefly.

Full on his foes, and aimed at Caesar's galley;
Withheld, he raves on you, cries he's betrayed.
Should he now find you—

ALEXAS.   Shun him; seek your safety
Till you can clear your innocence.

CLEOPATRA.   I'll stay.   105

ALEXAS.
You must not. Haste you to your monument,
While I make speed to Caesar.

CLEOPATRA.   Caesar! No,
I have no business with him.

ALEXAS.   I can work him
To spare your life, and let this madman perish.

CLEOPATRA.
Base, fawning wretch! wouldst thou betray him too?   110
Hence from my sight! I will not hear a traitor;
'Twas thy design brought all this ruin on us.—
Serapion, thou art honest. Counsel me;
But haste, each moment's precious.

SERAPION.
Retire; you must not yet see Antony.   115
He who began this mischief,
'Tis just he tempt the danger. Let him clear you;
And since he offered you his servile tongue
To gain a poor precarious life from Caesar,
Let him expose that fawning eloquence   120
And speak to Antony.

ALEXAS.   O heav'ns! I dare not;
I meet my certain death.

CLEOPATRA.   Slave, thou deserv'st it.
Not that I fear my lord, will I avoid him.
I know him noble: when he banished me
And thought me false, he scorned to take my life;   125
But I'll be justified, and then die with him.

102. at] *Q1–2; om. Q3,C1.*

---

106. *monument*] Cleopatra's partially completed mausoleum.

ALEXAS.

    O pity me, and let me follow you!

CLEOPATRA.

    To death, if thou stir hence. Speak, if thou canst,
    Now for thy life, which basely thou wouldst save,
    While mine I prize at—this! Come, good Serapion.   130

                Exeunt Cleopatra, Serapion, Charmion, Iras.

ALEXAS.

    O that I less could fear to lose this being,
    Which, like a snowball in my coward hand,
    The more 'tis grasped, the faster melts away.
    Poor reason! what a wretched aid art thou!
    For still, in spite of thee,   135
    These two long lovers, soul and body, dread
    Their final separation. Let me think:
    What can I say to save myself from death?
    No matter what becomes of Cleopatra.

ANTONY *(within)*.

    Which way? where?

VENTIDIUS *(within)*.   This leads to th'monument.   140

ALEXAS.

    Ah me! I hear him, yet I'm unprepared.
    My gift of lying's gone,
    And this court-devil, which I so oft have raised,
    Forsakes me at my need. I dare not stay,
    Yet cannot far go hence.   *Exit.* 145

        Enter Antony *and* Ventidius.

ANTONY.

    O happy Caesar! Thou hast men to lead:
    Think not 'tis thou hast conquered Antony,
    But Rome has conquered Egypt. I'm betrayed.

VENTIDIUS.

    Curse on this treach'rous train!
    Their soil and heav'n infect 'em all with baseness,   150
    And their young souls come tainted to the world
    With the first breath they draw.

ANTONY.

    Th'original villain sure no god created;

He was a bastard of the sun by Nile,
Aped into man, with all his mother's mud   155
Crusted about his soul.
VENTIDIUS.   The nation is
One universal traitor, and their queen
The very spirit and extract of 'em all.
ANTONY.
Is there yet left
A possibility of aid from valor?   160
Is there one god unsworn to my destruction?
The least unmortgaged hope? for if there be,
Methinks I cannot fall beneath the fate
Of such a boy as Caesar.
The world's one half is yet in Antony,   165
And from each limb of it that's hewed away
The soul comes back to me.
VENTIDIUS.   There yet remain
Three legions in the town; the last assault
Lopped off the rest. If death be your design—
As I must wish it now—these are sufficient   170
To make a heap about us of dead foes,
An honest pile for burial.
ANTONY.   They're enough.
We'll not divide our stars, but side by side
Fight emulous, and with malicious eyes
Survey each other's acts; so every death   175
Thou giv'st, I'll take on me as a just debt,
And pay thee back a soul.
VENTIDIUS.
Now you shall see I love you. Not a word
Of chiding more. By my few hours of life,
I am so pleased with this brave Roman fate   180
That I would not be Caesar, to outlive you.
When we put off this flesh and mount together,

---

154. *bastard . . . Nile*] bred by the sun from the mud of the Nile.
155. *Aped*] counterfeited.
165-167. *The . . . me*] explicated by H. Kossmann, "A Note on Dryden's
All for Love, V.165 ff.," *English Studies,* XXXI (1950), 99–100.

I shall be shown to all th'ethereal crowd:
"Lo, this is he who died with Antony!"

ANTONY.

Who knows but we may pierce through all their troops,   185
And reach my veterans yet? 'Tis worth the tempting
T'o'erleap this gulf of fate,
And leave our wond'ring destinies behind.

Enter Alexas, *trembling.*

VENTIDIUS.

See, see that villain!
See Cleopatra stamped upon that face,   190
With all her cunning, all her arts of falsehood!
How she looks out through those dissembling eyes!
How he has set his count'nance for deceit,
And promises a lie before he speaks!
Let me dispatch him first.   *Drawing.*

ALEXAS.   O spare me, spare me!   195

ANTONY.

Hold, he's not worth your killing. —On thy life,
Which thou mayst keep because I scorn to take it,
No syllable to justify thy queen;
Save thy base tongue its office.

ALEXAS.   Sir, she's gone
Where she shall never be molested more   200
By love, or you.

ANTONY.   Fled to her Dolabella!
Die, traitor! I revoke my promise! die!   *Going to kill him.*

ALEXAS.

O hold! she is not fled.

ANTONY.   She is; my eyes
Are open to her falsehood. My whole life
Has been a golden dream of love and friendship;   205
But now I wake, I'm like a merchant roused
From soft repose to see his vessel sinking,
And all his wealth cast o'er. Ingrateful woman!

188. wond'ring] *Q1*; wand'ring   193. has set] *Q1;* sets *Q2–3,C1.*
Q2–3,C1.

Who followed me but as the swallow summer,
Hatching her young ones in my kindly beams,   210
Singing her flatt'ries to my morning wake;
But now my winter comes, she spreads her wings,
And seeks the spring of Caesar.

ALEXAS.   Think not so:
Her fortunes have in all things mixed with yours.
Had she betrayed her naval force to Rome,   215
How easily might she have gone to Caesar,
Secure by such a bribe!

VENTIDIUS.   She sent it first,
To be more welcome after.

ANTONY.   'Tis too plain;
Else would she have appeared to clear herself.

ALEXAS.

Too fatally she has. She could not bear   220
To be accused by you, but shut herself
Within her monument; looked down and sighed,
While from her unchanged face the silent tears
Dropped, as they had not leave, but stole their parting.
Some undistinguished words she inly murmured;   225
At last she raised her eyes, and with such looks
As dying Lucrece cast—

ANTONY.   My heart forebodes—

VENTIDIUS.
All for the best; go on.

ALEXAS.   She snatched her poniard,
And, ere we could prevent the fatal blow,
Plunged it within her breast, then turned to me: 230
"Go, bear my lord," said she, "my last farewell,
And ask him if he yet suspect my faith."
More she was saying, but death rushed betwixt.
She half pronounced your name with her last breath,
And buried half within her.

VENTIDIUS.   Heav'n be praised!   235

---

212. spreads] *Q1,Q3,C1;* spread   217. bribe] *Q1,Q3,C1;* bride *Q2.*
Q2.

ANTONY.

    Then art thou innocent, my poor dear love,
    And art thou dead?
    O those two words! their sound should be divided:
    Hadst thou been false, and died; or hadst thou lived,
    And hadst been true— But innocence and death!   240
    This shows not well above. Then what am I,
    The murderer of this truth, this innocence?
    Thoughts cannot form themselves in words so horrid
    As can express my guilt!

VENTIDIUS.

    Is't come to this? The gods have been too gracious,   245
    And thus you thank 'em for't!

ANTONY *(to* Alexas).   Why stay'st thou here?

    Is it for thee to spy upon my soul
    And see its inward mourning? Get thee hence!
    Thou art not worthy to behold what now
    Becomes a Roman emp'ror to perform.   250

ALEXAS *(aside).*

    He loves her still:
    His grief betrays it. Good! The joy to find
    She's yet alive completes the reconcilement.
    I've saved myself and her. But, oh! the Romans!
    Fate comes too fast upon my wit,   255
    Hunts me too hard, and meets me at each double.   *Exit.*

VENTIDIUS.

    Would she had died a little sooner, though,
    Before Octavia went: you might have treated.
    Now 'twill look tame, and would not be received.
    Come, rouse yourself, and let's die warm together.   260

ANTONY.

    I will not fight: there's no more work for war.
    The business of my angry hours is done.

VENTIDIUS.

    Caesar is at your gates.

245. gracious] *Q1,Q3,C1;* graciou
Q2.

---

256. *double*] doubling back, like a hunted quarry.

ANTONY.   Why, let him enter;
    He's welcome now.
VENTIDIUS.
    What lethargy has crept into your soul?   265
ANTONY.
    'Tis but a scorn of life, and just desire
    To free myself from bondage.
VENTIDIUS.   Do it bravely.
ANTONY.
    I will; but not by fighting. O Ventidius!
    What should I fight for now? My queen is dead.
    I was but great for her; my pow'r, my empire   270
    Were but my merchandise to buy her love,
    And conquered kings, my factors. Now she's dead,
    Let Caesar take the world—
    An empty circle, since the jewel's gone
    Which made it worth my strife; my being's nauseous,   275
    For all the bribes of life are gone away.
VENTIDIUS.
    Would you be taken?
ANTONY.   Yes, I would be taken,
    But as a Roman ought—dead, my Ventidius;
    For I'll convey my soul from Caesar's reach,
    And lay down life myself. 'Tis time the world   280
    Should have a lord, and know whom to obey.
    We two have kept its homage in suspense,
    And bent the globe, on whose each side we trod,
    Till it was dinted inwards. Let him walk
    Alone upon't; I'm weary of my part.   285
    My torch is out, and the world stands before me
    Like a black desert at th'approach of night.
    I'll lay me down, and stray no farther on.
VENTIDIUS.
    I could be grieved,
    But that I'll not outlive you. Choose your death,   290
    For I have seen him in such various shapes,
    I care not which I take. I'm only troubled,

284. dinted] *Q1–3; dented C1.*

The life I bear is worn to such a rag,
'Tis scarce worth giving. I could wish, indeed,
We threw it from us with a better grace;   295
That like two lions taken in the toils,
We might at least thrust out our paws, and wound
The hunters that inclose us.

ANTONY.   I have thought on't.
Ventidius, you must live.

VENTIDIUS.   I must not, sir.

ANTONY.
Wilt thou not live to speak some good of me?   300
To stand by my fair fame, and guard th'approaches
From the ill tongues of men?

VENTIDIUS.   Who shall guard mine,
For living after you?

ANTONY.   Say, I command it.

VENTIDIUS.
If we die well, our deaths will speak themselves,
And need no living witness.

ANTONY.   Thou hast loved me,   305
And fain I would reward thee. I must die:
Kill me, and take the merit of my death
To make thee friends with Caesar.

VENTIDIUS.   Thank your kindness.
You said I loved you, and in recompense
You bid me turn a traitor. Did I think   310
You would have used me thus? that I should die
With a hard thought of you?

ANTONY.   Forgive me, Roman.
Since I have heard of Cleopatra's death,
My reason bears no rule upon my tongue,
But lets my thoughts break all at random out.   315
I've thought better; do not deny me twice.

VENTIDIUS.
By heav'n, I will not.
Let it not be t'outlive you.

ANTONY.   Kill me first,

297. least] *Q1;* last *Q2–3,C1.*

And then die thou; for 'tis but just thou serve
Thy friend before thyself.

VENTIDIUS.   Give me your hand.   320
We soon shall meet again. Now farewell, emperor! *Embrace.*
Methinks that word's too cold to be my last:
Since death sweeps all distinctions, farewell, friend!
That's all.—
I will not make a business of a trifle,   325
And yet I cannot look on you, and kill you;
Pray turn your face.

ANTONY.   I do. Strike home, be sure.

VENTIDIUS.

Home as my sword will reach.   *Kills himself.*

ANTONY.   Oh, thou mistak'st!
That wound was none of thine. Give it me back:
Thou robb'st me of my death.

VENTIDIUS.   I do, indeed.   330
But think, 'tis the first time I e'er deceived you,
If that may plead my pardon. —And you, gods,
Forgive me if you will, for I die perjured
Rather than kill my friend.   *Dies.*

ANTONY.

Farewell! Ever my leader, ev'n in death!   335
My queen and thou have got the start of me,
And I'm the lag of honor. —Gone so soon?
Is Death no more? He used him carelessly,
With a familiar kindness; ere he knocked,
Ran to the door and took him in his arms,   340
As who should say, "Y'are welcome at all hours,
A friend need give no warning." Books had spoiled him,
For all the learn'd are cowards by profession.
'Tis not worth
My farther thought, for death, for aught I know,   345
Is but to think no more. Here's to be satisfied.
                          Falls on his sword.
I've missed my heart. O unperforming hand!
Thou never couldst have erred in a worse time.

323. all] *Q1; om. Q2–3,C1.*   327. be] *Q1; om. Q2–3,C1.*

My fortune jades me to the last, and Death,
Like a great man, takes state, and makes me wait   350
For my admittance.—   *Trampling within.*
                    Some, perhaps, from Caesar.
If he should find me living, and suspect
That I played booty with my life! I'll mend
My work ere they can reach me.   *Rises upon his knees.*

          Enter Cleopatra, Charmion, Iras.

CLEOPATRA.
Where is my lord? where is he?
CHARMION.   There he lies,   355
And dead Ventidius by him.
CLEOPATRA.
My fears were prophets; I am come too late.
O that accurst Alexas!   *Runs to him.*
ANTONY.   Art thou living?
Or am I dead before I knew, and thou
The first kind ghost that meets me?
CLEOPATRA.   Help me seat him. 360
Send quickly, send for help!   *They place him in a chair.*
ANTONY.   I am answered:
We live both. Sit thee down, my Cleopatra;
I'll make the most I can of life, to stay
A moment more with thee.
CLEOPATRA.
How is it with you?
ANTONY.   'Tis as with a man   365
Removing in a hurry, all packed up
But one dear jewel that his haste forgot,
And he, for that, returns upon the spur:
So I come back for thee.

358.S.D. *Runs to him.*] *Q1–3; om.*
C1.

---

350. *takes state*] stands on ceremony.
353. *played booty*] deliberately played badly at first, like a false game-ster, in order to cheat his victim eventually.

CLEOPATRA.

Too long, you heav'ns, you have been cruel to me; 370
Now show your mended faith, and give me back
His fleeting life!

ANTONY.   It will not be, my love.
I keep my soul by force.
Say but thou art not false.

CLEOPATRA.   'Tis now too late
To say I'm true: I'll prove it, and die with you. 375
Unknown to me, Alexas feigned my death;
Which when I knew, I hasted to prevent
This fatal consequence. My fleet betrayed
Both you and me.

ANTONY.   And Dolabella?

CLEOPATRA.   Scarce
Esteemed before he loved, but hated now. 380

ANTONY.

Enough. My life's not long enough for more.
Thou say'st thou wilt come after: I believe thee,
For I can now believe whate'er thou say'st,
That we may part more kindly.

CLEOPATRA.   I will come.
Doubt not, my life, I'll come, and quickly too: 385
Caesar shall triumph o'er no part of thee.

ANTONY.

But grieve not, while thou stay'st
My last disastrous times:
Think we have had a clear and glorious day,
And heav'n did kindly to delay the storm 390
Just till our close of ev'ning. Ten years' love,
And not a moment lost, but all improved
To th'utmost joys—what ages have we lived!
And now to die each other's; and so dying,
While hand in hand we walk in groves below, 395
Whole troops of lovers' ghosts shall flock about us,
And all the train be ours.

379–380. Scarce . . . now] *printed
as one line in Q1–3,C1.*

CLEOPATRA.

    Your words are like the notes of dying swans,
    Too sweet to last. Were there so many hours
    For your unkindness, and not one for love?   400

ANTONY.

    No, not a minute. —This one kiss—more worth
    Than all I leave to Caesar.   *Dies.*

CLEOPATRA.

    O tell me so again,
    And take ten thousand kisses for that word.
    My lord, my lord! Speak, if you yet have being.   405
    Sigh to me, if you cannot speak, or cast
    One look! Do anything that shows you live.

IRAS.

    He's gone too far to hear you,
    And this you see, a lump of senseless clay,
    The leavings of a soul.

CHARMION.   Remember, madam,   410

    He charged you not to grieve.

CLEOPATRA.   And I'll obey him.

    I have not loved a Roman not to know
    What should become his wife—his wife, my Charmion!
    For 'tis to that high title I aspire,
    And now I'll not die less. Let dull Octavia   415
    Survive, to mourn him dead; my nobler fate
    Shall knit our spousals with a tie too strong
    For Roman laws to break.

IRAS.   Will you then die?

CLEOPATRA.

    Why shouldst thou make that question?

IRAS.

    Caesar is merciful.

CLEOPATRA.   Let him be so   420

    To those that want his mercy; my poor lord
    Made no such cov'nant with him to spare me
    When he was dead. Yield me to Caesar's pride?

398. swans] *Q1–2;* swan *Q3,C1.*   420. merciful] *Q1;* most merciful
413. become] *Q1;* become of *Q2–3,*   *Q2–3,C1.*
C1.

What! to be led in triumph through the streets,
A spectacle to base plebeian eyes,   425
While some dejected friend of Antony's,
Close in a corner, shakes his head and mutters
A secret curse on her who ruined him?
I'll none of that.

CHARMION.   Whatever you resolve,
I'll follow ev'n to death.

IRAS.   I only feared   430
For you, but more should fear to live without you.

CLEOPATRA.

Why, now 'tis as it should be. Quick, my friends,
Dispatch; ere this, the town's in Caesar's hands.
My lord looks down concerned, and fears my stay,
Lest I should be surprised;   435
Keep him not waiting for his love too long.
You, Charmion, bring my crown and richest jewels;
With 'em, the wreath of victory I made
(Vain augury!) for him who now lies dead.
You, Iras, bring the cure of all our ills.   440

IRAS.

The aspics, madam?

CLEOPATRA.   Must I bid you twice?

                              Exeunt Charmion *and* Iras.
'Tis sweet to die when they would force life on me;
To rush into the dark abode of Death,
And seize him first. If he be like my love,
He is not frightful, sure.   445
We're now alone, in secrecy and silence,
And is not this like lovers? I may kiss
These pale, cold lips; Octavia does not see me,
And, oh! 'tis better far to have him thus
Than see him in her arms. —Oh, welcome, welcome!   450

Enter Charmion, Iras.

CHARMION.

What must be done?

CLEOPATRA.   Short ceremony, friends,
   But yet it must be decent. First, this laurel
   Shall crown my hero's head: he fell not basely,
   Nor left his shield behind him. —Only thou
   Couldst triumph o'er thyself, and thou alone   455
   Wert worthy so to triumph.
CHARMION.   To what end
   These ensigns of your pomp and royalty?
CLEOPATRA.
   Dull that thou art! Why, 'tis to meet my love
   As when I saw him first, on Cydnos' bank,
   All sparkling like a goddess. So adorned,   460
   I'll find him once again; my second spousals
   Shall match my first in glory. Haste, haste, both,
   And dress the bride of Antony.
CHARMION.   'Tis done.
CLEOPATRA.
   Now seat me by my lord. I claim this place,
   For I must conquer Caesar too, like him,   465
   And win my share o'th' world. —Hail, you dear relics
   Of my immortal love!
   Oh, let no impious hand remove you hence,
   But rest forever here! Let Egypt give
   His death that peace which it denied his life.—   470
   Reach me the casket.
IRAS.   Underneath the fruit
   The aspic lies.
CLEOPATRA *(putting aside the leaves).*
             Welcome, thou kind deceiver!
   Thou best of thieves, who, with an easy key,
   Dost open life, and unperceived by us,

---

469. here] *Q1–2,C1;* her *Q3.*   471–472. Underneath . . . lies]
                            printed as one line in Q1–3,C1.

---

454. *his shield*] perhaps echoing the Spartan mother's proverbial
exhortation to her son to return with his shield or on it.
459. *Cydnos*] See III.162, and note.

Ev'n steal us from ourselves; discharging so   475
Death's dreadful office better than himself;
Touching our limbs so gently into slumber
That Death stands by, deceived by his own image,
And thinks himself but Sleep.
SERAPION *(within)*.   The queen, where is she?
The town is yielded, Caesar's at the gates.   480
CLEOPATRA.

He comes too late t'invade the rights of death.
Haste, bare my arm, and rouse the serpent's fury.

              Holds out her arm, and draws it back.

Coward flesh,
Wouldst thou conspire with Caesar to betray me,
As thou wert none of mine? I'll force thee to't,   485
And not be sent by him,
But bring, myself, my soul to Antony.

          Turns aside, and then shows her arm bloody.

Take hence; the work is done.
SERAPION *(within)*.   Break ope the door,
And guard the traitor well.
CHARMION.   The next is ours.
IRAS.

Now, Charmion, to be worthy   490
Of our great queen and mistress.   *They apply the aspics.*
CLEOPATRA.

Already, death, I feel thee in my veins.
I go with such a will to find my lord
That we shall quickly meet.
A heavy numbness creeps through every limb,   495
And now 'tis at my head; my eyelids fall,
And my dear love is vanished in a mist.

491. our] *Q1;* your *Q2–3,C1.*

---

475. *steal . . . ourselves*] derived from Daniel's description of death
as "gentle cunning thief/ That from ourselves so steal'st ourselves
away" (*The Tragedie of Cleopatra*, V.1536–1537), and a source of
Pope's "Years following years, steal something every day;/ At last
they steal us from ourselves away" (*Imitations of Horace, Epistles*
II.ii.72–73).

Where shall I find him, where? O turn me to him,
And lay me on his breast! —Caesar, thy worst.
Now part us, if thou canst.   *Dies.*

Iras *sinks down at her feet and dies;* Charmion *stands behind her chair, as dressing her head. Enter* Serapion, Two Priests, Alexas *bound, Egyptians.*

TWO PRIESTS.   Behold, Serapion,   500
    What havoc death has made!
SERAPION.   'Twas what I feared—
    Charmion, is this well done?
CHARMION.
    Yes, 'tis well done, and like a queen, the last
    Of her great race. I follow her.   *Sinks down; dies.*
ALEXAS.   'Tis true,
    She has done well. Much better thus to die   505
    Than live to make a holiday in Rome.
SERAPION.
    See, see how th'lovers sit in state together,
    As they were giving laws to half mankind!
    Th'impression of a smile, left in her face,
    Shows she died pleased with him for whom she lived,   510
    And went to charm him in another world.
    Caesar's just ent'ring: grief has now no leisure.
    Secure that villain as our pledge of safety
    To grace th'imperial triumph. —Sleep, blest pair,
    Secure from human chance, long ages out,   515
    While all the storms of fate fly o'er your tomb;
            And fame to late posterity shall tell,
            No lovers lived so great, or died so well.

498. Where shall] *Q1–2,C1;* Were   506. Rome] *Q1–2;* Roman *Q3,C1.*
shall *Q3.*   516. o'er] *Q1–2,C1;* e'er *Q3.*
500–501. Behold . . . made]
printed as one line in Q1–3,C1.

EPILOGUE

Poets, like disputants when reasons fail,
Have one sure refuge left—and that's to rail.
Fop, coxcomb, fool, are thundered through the pit,
And this is all their equipage of wit.
We wonder how the devil this diff'rence grows   5
Betwixt our fools in verse, and yours in prose;
For, 'faith, the quarrel rightly understood,
'Tis civil war with their own flesh and blood.
The threadbare author hates the gaudy coat,
And swears at the gilt coach, but swears afoot;   10
For 'tis observed of every scribbling man,
He grows a fop as fast as e'er he can:
Prunes up, and asks his oracle, the glass,
If pink or purple best become his face.
For our poor wretch, he neither rails nor prays,   15
Nor likes your wit just as you like his plays:
He has not yet so much of Mr. Bayes.
He does his best, and if he cannot please,
Would quietly sue out his writ of ease.
Yet, if he might his own grand jury call,   20
By the fair sex he begs to stand or fall.
Let Caesar's pow'r the men's ambition move,
But grace you him who lost the world for love!
Yet if some antiquated lady say
The last age is not copied in his play,   25
Heav'n help the man who for that face must drudge,
Which only has the wrinkles of a judge.
Let not the young and beauteous join with those,
For should you raise such num'rous hosts of foes,
Young wits and sparks he to his aid must call: 30
'Tis more than one man's work to please you all.

2. refuge] *Q1,Q3,C1;* refurge *Q2.*   30. sparks] *Q1,Q3,C1;* sparke *Q2.*
13. his oracle, the] *Q1–3;* the
oracle, his *C1.*

17. *Mr. Bayes*] a character satirizing Dryden in Buckingham's *The Rehearsal.*
19. *writ of ease*] certificate of discharge from employment.

Appendix A

Copies Collated

The following copies of *All for Love* were collated for all substantive variants:

Q1: (1) University of Illinois Library (I). (2) Folger Shakespeare Library (F); Wing D2229; Cs. 163; Caracciolo[1] copy m. (3) Pierpont Morgan Library (PM); PML 36682; bookplate of A. Edward Newton. (4) British Museum (BM); T 1945(4); Caracciolo copy B. (5) Bodleian Library (B); 1678. MAL. B. 288(1); Caracciolo copy F.

Q2: (1) U. of Illinois (I). (2) Folger (F); Wing D2230; Cs. 753; initials of J. P. Kemble, 1798; Devonshire-Huntington copy.

Q3: (1) U. of Illinois. (2) Folger; Wing 2231; Cs. 133.

C1: (1) U. of Illinois; xq822. D84. cop. 3; Alexander Pope's copy. (2) Folger; PR 3410. 1701 Cage; autographs of Mary S. Douglas and Norman Wilkinson.

Q4: Folger; PR 3416. A6 Cage; H. Buxton Forman copy.

Q5: University of Texas Library; Aj. D848. 678ae.

C2: Folger; PR 3416. A1 1717 Cage.

The following stop-press variants were detected in Q1:[2]

	Uncorrected	*Corrected*
	Sheet B (inner forme)	
Copies	B	I, F, PM, BM
Sig. B2r, l. 23	perish, here,	perish, perish,
	Sheet F (outer forme)	
Copies	I, F, BM	PM, B
Sig. F1r, l. 35	Ventidius,	Ventidius, *and*

---

[1] Peter Caracciolo, "Some Unrecorded Variants in the First Edition of Dryden's *All for Love*, 1678," *The Book Collector*, XIII (1964), 498–500.

[2] L. A. Beaurline and Fredson Bowers claim to have found a stop-press variant (proper;/proper,) in sig. b2v, l. 8 (*John Dryden: Four Tragedies*, Chicago, 1967, p. 280).

Sheet K (outer forme)

Copies	F, BM	I, PM, B
Sig. K1r, l. 29	cam'st	com'st
Sig. K1r, l. 33	share	spare
Sig. K2v, l. 23	As . . . now,	(As . . . now)
Sig. K2v, l. 30	givest	giv'st
Sig. K2v, l. 31	in	back

Additional stop-press variants were detected in Q2, Sheet B (outer forme):

Copies	I	F
Sig. B2v, l. 34	stflied	stifled
Sig. B3r, l. 9	)for	(for
Sig. B3r, l. 10	degre	degree
Sig. B3r, l. 31	*Tu ui*	*Tum*

Appendix B

Chronology

Approximate dates are indicated by*. Dates for plays are those on which they were first made public, either on stage or in print.

Political and Literary Events	*Life and Major Works of Dryden*
1631 Death of Donne.	Born in Aldwinckle, Northamptonshire, August 9.
1633 Samuel Pepys born.	
1635 Sir George Etherege born.*	
1640 Aphra Behn born.*	
1641 William Wycherley born.*	
1642 First Civil War began (ended 1646). Theaters closed by Parliament. Thomas Shadwell born.*	
1646	Became a King's Scholar at Westminster School, London.*
1648 Second Civil War. Nathaniel Lee born.*	
1649 Execution of Charles I.	*Upon the Death of the Lord Hastings* published.
1650 Jeremy Collier born.	Admitted to Trinity College, Cambridge, on May 18. *To John Hoddeston, on His Divine Epigrams* published.

1651

Hobbes's *Leviathan* published.

1652

First Dutch War began (ended 1654).

Thomas Otway born.

1654

B.A., left Cambridge in March. His father died in June.

1656

D'Avenant's *THE SIEGE OF RHODES* performed at Rutland House.

Employed by Cromwell's government (until 1658).

1657

John Dennis born.

1658

Death of Oliver Cromwell.

D'Avenant's *THE CRUELTY OF THE SPANIARDS IN PERU* performed at the Cockpit.

1659

Heroic Stanzas to the Glorious Memory of Cromwell published.

1660

Restoration of Charles II.

Theatrical patents granted to Thomas Killigrew and Sir William D'Avenant, authorizing them to form, respectively, the King's and the Duke of York's Companies.

Pepys began his diary.

To My Honored Friend, Sir Robbert Howard and *Astraea Redux* published (June).

1661

Cowley's *THE CUTTER OF COLEMAN STREET*.

D'Avenant's *THE SIEGE OF RHODES* (e x p a n d e d to two parts.)

To His Sacred Majesty, A Panegyric on His Coronation published (April).

1662

Charter granted to the Royal Society.

Publication of *To My Lord Chancellor* (January 1) and *To My*

Honored Friend, Dr. Charleton
(September*).
Elected a Fellow of the Royal
Society (November 19).

1663
Tuke's *THE ADVENTURES OF
FIVE HOURS.*

THE WILD GALLANT (Vere
Street, February 5).
Married Lady Elizabeth Howard
(December 1).

1664
Sir John Vanbrugh born.
Etherege's *THE COMICAL RE-
VENGE.*

THE INDIAN QUEEN, with Sir
Robert Howard (Bridges Street,
January 25).
THE RIVAL LADIES (Bridges
Street, June).

1665
Second Dutch War began (ended
1667).
Great Plague.
Orrery's *MUSTAPHA.*

*THE INDIAN EMPEROR, OR
THE CONQUEST OF MEXICO
BY THE SPANIARDS* (Bridges
Street, April).

1666
Fire of London.
Death of James Shirley.

Eldest son, Charles, born (August
27).

1667
Jonathan Swift born.
Milton's *Paradise Lost* published.
Sprat's *The History of the Royal
Society* published.

Annus Mirabilis published (Jan-
uary).
*S E C R E T   LOVE,   OR   THE
MAIDEN QUEEN* (Bridges Street,
March 2).
*SIR   MARTIN   MAR-ALL,   OR
THE   FEIGNED   INNOCENCE*
(Lincoln's Inn Fields, August 15).
*THE TEMPEST, OR THE EN-
CHANTED ISLAND,* with D'Ave-
nant (Lincoln's Inn Fields, No-
vember 7).

1668
Death of D'Avenant.
Shadwell's *THE SULLEN LOV-
ERS.*
Etherege's *SHE WOULD IF SHE
COULD.*

Second son, John, born.
Appointed Poet Laureate (April).
An Essay of Dramatic Poesy pub-
lished (May or June).
*AN EVENING'S LOVE, OR THE
MOCK ASTROLOGER* (Bridges
Street, June 12).
Awarded honorary M.A. degree
(June 17).

– 137 –

1669
Pepys terminated his diary.
Susanna Centlivre born.

Third son, Erasmus-Henry, born (May 2).
TYRANNIC LOVE, OR THE ROYAL MARTYR (Bridges Street, June 24).

1670
William Congreve born.

Appointed Historiographer Royal (July).
THE CONQUEST OF GRANADA BY THE SPANIARDS, Part I (Bridges Street, December).

1671
Dorset Garden Theatre (Duke's Company) opened.
Colley Cibber born.
Milton's *Paradise Regained* and *Samson Agonistes* published.
THE REHEARSAL, by the Duke of Buckingham and others.
Wycherley's *LOVE IN A WOOD.*

THE CONQUEST OF GRANADA, Part II (Bridges Street, January).

1672
Third Dutch War began (ended 1674).
Joseph Addison born.
Richard Steele born.

MARRIAGE A LA MODE (Lincoln's Inn Fields, April*).
THE ASSIGNATION, OR LOVE IN A NUNNERY (Lincoln's Inn Fields, November).

1673

AMBOYNA (Lincoln's Inn Fields, May).

1674
New Drury Lane Theatre (King's Company) opened.
Death of Milton.
Nicholas Rowe born.
Thomas Rymer's *Reflections on Aristotle's Treatise of Poesy* (translation of Rapin) published.

1675
Wycherley's *THE COUNTRY WIFE.*

AURENG-ZEBE (Drury Lane, November 17).

1676
Etherege's *THE MAN OF MODE.*
Otway's *DON CARLOS.*

Mac Flecknoe written (July or later).

Shadwell's *THE VIRTUOSO.*
Wycherley's *THE PLAIN DEALER.*

1677
Aphra Behn's *THE ROVER.*
Lee's *THE RIVAL QUEENS.*
Rymer's *Tragedies of the Last Age Considered* published.

THE STATE OF INNOCENCE AND FALL OF MAN published (February).
ALL FOR LOVE, OR THE WORLD WELL LOST (Drury Lane, December 12).

1678
Popish Plot.
George Farquhar born.
Bunyan's *Pilgrim's Progress* (Part I) published.

THE KIND KEEPER, OR MR. LIMBERHAM (Dorset Garden, March 11).
OEDIPUS, with Nathaniel Lee (Dorset Garden, September*).

1679
Exclusion Bill introduced.
Death of Thomas Hobbes.
Death of Roger Boyle, Earl of Orrery.
Charles Johnson born.

TROILUS AND CRESSIDA, OR TRUTH FOUND TOO LATE (Dorset Garden, April*).
Beaten by hired thugs in Rose Alley on the night of December 18.

1680
Death of Samuel Butler.
Death of John Wilmot, Earl of Rochester.
Lee's *LUCIUS JUNIUS BRUTUS.*
Otway's *THE ORPHAN.*

Ovid's Epistles published (February).
THE SPANISH FRIAR, OR THE DOUBLE DISCOVERY (Dorset Garden, November 1*).

1681
Charles II dissolved Parliament at Oxford.
Tate's adaptation of *KING LEAR.*

Publication of *His Majesty's Declaration Defended* (June) and *Absalom and Achitophel,* Part I (November).

1682
The King's and the Duke of York's Companies merged into the United Company.
Otway's *VENICE PRESERVED.*

Publication of *The Medal* (March), *Mac Flecknoe* (October), *Absalom and Achitophel,* Part II (November), and *Religio Laici* (November).
THE DUKE OF GUISE, with Lee (Drury Lane, November 28).

1683
Rye House Plot.
Death of Thomas Killigrew.

Publication of *Vindication of the Duke of Guise* (April*) and trans-

Crowne's *CITY POLITIQUES*.

1684

1685

Death of Charles II; accession of James II.
Revocation of the Edict of Nantes.
The Duke of Monmouth's Rebellion.
Death of Otway.
John Gay born.
Crowne's *SIR COURTLY NICE*.

1686

1687

Death of the Duke of Buckingham.
Newton's *Principia* published.

1688

The Revolution.
Alexander Pope born.
Shadwell's *THE S Q U I R E OF ALSATIA*.

1689

The War of the League of Augsburg began (ended 1697).
Toleration Act.
Death of Aphra Behn.
Shadwell made Poet Laureate.
Shadwell's *BURY FAIR*.

1690

Battle of the Boyne.
Locke's *Two Treatises of Government* and *An Essay Concerning Human Understanding* published.

lation of *Plutarch's Lives* (April or May).

Publication of *Miscellany Poems* (February), translation of Maimbourg's *History of the League* (July), and *To the Memory of Mr. Oldham*.

Publication of *Sylvae* (January), *Threnodia Augustalis* (March), and *To the Pious Memory of Mrs. Anne Killigrew* (November). *ALBION AND ALBANIUS* (Dorset Garden, June 3).
Became a Roman Catholic.

A Defence of the Papers Written by the Late King of Blessed Memory and Duchess of York published (July).

The Hind and the Panther published (May).
A Song for St. Cecilia's Day, 1687 (November 22).

Publication of *Britannia Rediviva* (June) and translation of Bouhours's *Life of St. Francis Xavier* (July).

DON SEBASTIAN, KING OF PORTUGAL (Drury Lane, December 4).

AMPHITRYON, OR THE TWO SOSIAS, with music by Henry Purcell (Drury Lane, October 21).

1691
Death of Etherege.*
Langbaine's *An Account of the English Dramatic Poets* published.
1692
Death of Lee.
Death of Shadwell.
Tate made Poet Laureate.

1693
George Lillo born.*
Rymer's *A Short View of Tragedy* published.
Congreve's THE OLD BACHELOR.
1694
Death of Queen Mary.
Southerne's THE FATAL MARRIAGE.

1695
Group of actors led by Thomas Betterton left Drury Lane and established a new company at Lincoln's Inn Fields.
Congreve's *LOVE FOR LOVE.*
Southerne's *OROONOKO.*

1696
Cibber's *LOVE'S LAST SHIFT.*
Vanbrugh's *THE RELAPSE.*
1697
Treaty of Ryswick ended the War of the League of Augsburg.
Charles Macklin born.
Congreve's THE MOURNING BRIDE.
Vanbrugh's THE PROVOKED WIFE.
1698
Collier controversy started with the publication of *A Short View of the Immorality and Profaneness of the English Stage.*

KING ARTHUR, OR THE BRITISH WORTHY, with music by Purcell (Dorset Garden, May).

Publication of *Eleonora* (March) and *The Satires of Juvenal and Persius* (October).
CLEOMENES, THE SPARTAN HERO (Drury Lane, April).

Publication of *Examen Poeticum* (July) and *To My Dear Friend, Mr. Congreve* (December).

LOVE TRIUMPHANT, OR NATURE WILL PREVAIL (Drury Lane, January).
The Annual Miscellany, for the Year 1694 published (June).

Translation of Du Fresnoy's *Art of Painting* published (July).

An Ode on the Death of Mr. Henry Purcell published (June*).

Translation of Virgil published (August).
Alexander's Feast (November 22).

1699
Farquhar's *T H E   CONSTANT*
COUPLE.

1700
Blackmore's *Satire against Wit*
published.
Congreve's *THE WAY OF THE*
WORLD.

1701
Act of Settlement.
War of the Spanish Succession
began (ended 1713).
Death of James II.
Rowe's *TAMERLANE.*
Steele's *THE FUNERAL.*

1702
Death of William III; accession
of Anne.
The Daily Courant began publi-
cation.
Cibber's *SHE   W O U L D   AND*
SHE WOULD NOT.

1703
Death of Samuel Pepys.
Rowe's *THE FAIR PENITENT.*

1704
Capture of Gibraltar; Battle of
Blenheim.
Defoe's *The Review* began publi-
cation (1704–1713).
Swift's *A Tale of a Tub* and *The*
Battle of the Books published.
Cibber's *THE CARELESS HUS-*
BAND.

1705
Haymarket Theatre opened.
Steele's *THE   TENDER   HUS-*
BAND.

1706
Battle of Ramillies.
Farquhar's *THE RECRUITING*
OFFICER.

1707
Union of Scotland and England.
Death of Farquhar.

Fables Ancient and Modern published (March).
Died in London, May 1.

Henry Fielding born.
Farquhar's *THE BEAUX' STRATAGEM*.

1708
Downes's *Roscius Anglicanus* published.

1709
Samuel Johnson born.
Rowe's edition of Shakespeare published.
The Tatler began publication (1709–1711).
Centlivre's *THE BUSY BODY*.

1711
Shaftesbury's *Characteristics* published.
The Spectator began publication (1711–1712).
Pope's *An Essay on Criticism* published.

1713
Treaty of Utrecht ended the War of the Spanish Succession.
Addison's *CATO*.

1714
Death of Anne; accession of George I.
Steele became Governor of Drury Lane.
John Rich assumed management of Lincoln's Inn Fields.
Centlivre's *THE WONDER: A WOMAN KEEPS A SECRET*.
Rowe's *JANE SHORE*.

1715
Jacobite Rebellion.
Death of Tate.
Rowe made Poet Laureate.
Death of Wycherley.

1716
Addison's *THE DRUMMER*.

1717
David Garrick born.
Cibber's *THE NON-JUROR*.

Gay, P o p e, and Arbuthnot's
*THREE HOURS AFTER MAR-
RIAGE*.

1718
Death of Rowe.
Centlivre's *A BOLD STROKE
FOR A WIFE*.

1719
Death of Addison.
Defoe's *Robinson Crusoe* pub-
lished.
Young's *BUSIRIS, KING OF
EGYPT*.

1720
South Sea Bubble.
Samuel Foote born.
Steele suspended from the Gover-
norship of Drury Lane (restored
1721).
Little Theatre in the Haymarket
opened.
Steele's *The Theatre* (periodical)
published.
Hughes's *THE SIEGE OF DA-
MASCUS*.

1721
Walpole became first Minister.

1722
Steele's *THE C O N S C I O U S
LOVERS*.

1723
Death of Susanna Centlivre.
Death of D'Urfey.

1725
Pope's edition of Shakespeare
published.

1726
Death of Jeremy Collier.
Death of Vanbrugh.
Law's *Unlawfulness of Stage En-
tertainments* published.
Swift's *Gulliver's Travels* pub-
lished.

1727
Death of George I; accession of

George II.
Death of Sir Isaac Newton.
Arthur Murphy born.

1728
Pope's *The Dunciad* (first version)
published.
Cibber's *THE PROVOKED HUS-
BAND* (expansion of Vanbrugh's
fragment *A JOURNEY TO LON-
DON*).
Gay's *THE BEGGAR'S OPERA*.

1729
Goodman's Fields Theatre opened.
Death of Congreve.
Death of Steele.
Edmund Burke born.

1730
Cibber made Poet Laureate.
Oliver Goldsmith born.
Thomson's *The Seasons* published.
Fielding's *THE A U T H O R ' S
FARCE*.
Fielding's *TOM THUMB* (revised
as *THE TRAGEDY OF TRAGE-
DIES*, 1731).

1731
Death of Defoe.
Fielding's *THE GRUB-STREET
OPERA*.
Lillo's *THE LONDON MER-
CHANT*.

1732
Covent Garden Theatre opened.
Death of Gay.
George Colman the elder born.
Fielding's *THE COVENT GAR-
DEN TRAGEDY*.
Fielding's *THE MODERN HUS-
BAND*.
Charles Johnson's *CAELIA*.

1733
Pope's *An Essay on Man* (Epistles
I–III) published (Epistle IV,
1734).

1734
Death of Dennis.
The Prompter began publication
(1734–1736).
Theobald's edition of Shakes-
peare published.
Fielding's *DON QUIXOTE IN
ENGLAND.*

1736
Fielding led the "Great Mogul's
Company of Comedians" at the
Little Theatre in the Haymarket
(1736–1737).
Fielding's *PASQUIN.*
Lillo's *FATAL CURIOSITY.*

1737
The Stage Licensing Act.
Dodsley's *THE KING AND THE
MILLER OF MANSFIELD.*
Fielding's *THE HISTORICAL
REGISTER FOR THE YEAR
1736.*